Houghton Mifflin

California Math

Homework and Problem Solving

Student Book

- **Homework**
- **Leveled Problem Solving**

GRADE **4**

 HOUGHTON MIFFLIN   BOSTON

ISBN 10: 0-618-96130-5
ISBN 13: 978-0-618-96130-6

5 6 7 8 9 1429 16 15 14 13 12 11 10 09

Hands On: How Big Is 1 Million?

CA Standard
KEY NS 1.1

Use the chart to answer the following questions.

> **How many tens are in 1,000,000?**
>
> **Step 1** Read through the chart to find an equation involving tens and 1 million.
>
> **Step 2** Find the line on the left-hand side of the chart that lists the equation 10 × 100,000 = 1,000,000. Read the right-hand side to make sure that this equation relates to both tens and 1 million.
>
> **Step 3** Identify the number multiplied by 10 to find 1 million.
>
> | | |
> |---|---|
> | 1 × 1,000,000 = 1,000,000 ⟶ | 1 times 1 million = 1 million |
> | 10 × 100,000 = 1,000,000 ⟶ | 10 times 1 hundred thousand = 1 million |
> | 100 × 10,000 = 1,000,000 ⟶ | 100 times 10 thousand = 1 million |
> | 1,000 × 1,000 = 1,000,000 ⟶ | 1,000 times 1 thousand = 1 million |
> | 10,000 × 100 = 1,000,000 ⟶ | 10,000 times 1 hundred = 1 million |
> | 100,000 × 10 = 1,000,000 ⟶ | 100,000 times ten = 1 million |
> | 1,000,000 × 1 = 1,000,000 ⟶ | 1,000,000 times 1 = 1 million |
>
> **Solution:** There are 100,000 tens in 1,000,000.

1. How many ones are there in 1,000,000? _____

2. How many hundreds are there in 1,000,000? _____

3. How many hundred thousands are in 1,000,000? _____

4. How many ten thousands are there in 1,000,000? _____

5. How many thousands are there in 1,000,000? _____

Spiral Review (Grade 3, Chapter 2, Lesson 3) **NS 1.4, NS 1.3**

Round each number to the nearest ten and the nearest hundred.

6. 662 _____   **7.** 946 _____

8. Harriet has 247 beads of various colors. Her goal is to have about twice as many beads as this before she begins to make a complicated necklace. If she rounds 247 to the nearest ten before doubling the number, about how many beads will she use in all?

_____

Homework
1
Use with text pp. 6–7

Hands On: How Big Is 1 Million?

CA Standard
KEY NS 1.1

Solve.

1. A man and woman won a prize of $1,000,000. Soon they will receive a check for that amount. However, if they chose to take payment in one-dollar bills, how many bills would they receive in all?

2. A long-distance telephone company has 1 million customers. On Monday, each of these customers makes 1 telephone call. How many telephone calls are placed by the company's customers that day?

3. A bank teller is putting pennies in rolls. Each roll holds 100 pennies and the bank teller has 1,000,000 pennies. How many rolls will the teller need for all of the pennies?

4. A sorting machine at the post office divides 1,000,000 letters into 10 equal groups. How many letters are there in each group?

5. Rudy makes a list of cities that have a population of 100,000. How many of these cities would Rudy need to list to make a total population of 1 million?

6. A factory manufactures thumbtacks. Small boxes of thumbtacks are placed in larger shipping cartons in the warehouse. Each shipping carton contains 1,000 thumbtacks. If there are 1 million thumbtacks in the warehouse, how many cartons are there?

Place Value Through Hundred Thousands

CA Standard
NS 1.0

Write 328 thousand, 514 in two different ways.

Step 1 Look at the number and decide how many periods it contains. Reading from the left, say the number aloud.

Step 2 Write the number in word form.
Three hundred twenty-eight thousand, five hundred fourteen.

Step 3 Write the number in standard form.
328,514

Write each number in two other ways.

1. 246 thousand, 718

_____

_____

_____

2. 342 thousand, 159

_____

_____

_____

Write the value of the underlined digit.

3. 76,9_8_2 _____   **4.** 6_6_,424 _____   **5.** 925,7_3_3 _____

Spiral Review (Chapter 1, Lesson 1) **KEY NS 1.1**

Answer the following questions.

6. How many ones are there in 1 million? _____

7. How many hundreds are there in 1 million? _____

8. A media company divides 1 million copies of a new music CD into 100 equal groups before shipping the CDs to 100 stores. How many CDs is the company shipping to each store?

_____

Place Value Through Hundred Thousands

CA Standard
KEY NS 1.0

Solve.

1. What is the value of the underlined digit in the number 410,<u>3</u>27?

   _____

2. How do you write two hundred seventy-five thousand in standard form?

   _____

3. How do you write five hundred ninety-three thousand, seven hundred forty in standard form?

   _____

4. What is the value of the underlined digit in the number 26<u>4</u>,681?

   _____

5. How do you write six hundred four thousand, twenty-seven in standard form?

   _____

6. What is the value of the underlined digit in the number 8<u>0</u>9,425?

   _____

4
Use with text pp. 8–10

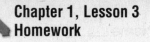
Place Value Through Hundred Millions

CA Standard
KEY NS 1.1

Write 328 million, 541 thousand, 670 in two ways.

Step ❶ Look at the number and decide how many periods it contains. Reading from the left, say the number aloud.

Step ❷ Write the number in word form.
Three hundred twenty-eight million, five hundred forty-one thousand, six hundred seventy.

Step ❸ Write the number in standard form.
328,541,670

Write each number in two other ways.

1. 612 million, 483 thousand, 125

_____

_____

2. 105 million, 602 thousand, 950

_____

_____

Write the value of the underlined digit.

3. 3_7_,295,810 _____   **4.** 4_9_6,021,795 _____   **5.** _6_38,912,004 _____

Spiral Review   (Chapter 1, Lesson 2) **NS 1.0**

Write each number in word form.

6. 452,859 _____

_____

7. 283,107 _____

_____

8. What is the value of the underlined digit in the number 385,5_2_6?

_____

Place Value Through Hundred Millions

Solve.

1. What is the value of the underlined digit in the number 539,7<u>2</u>1,004?

   _____

2. How do you write fifty-one million in standard form?

   _____

3. How do you write two hundred four million, three hundred ninety-eight thousand, two hundred in standard form?

   _____

4. What is the value of the underlined digit in the number 3<u>1</u>0,552,012?

   _____

5. How do you write one hundred one million, two hundred thirty thousand, four in standard form?

   _____

6. What are the values of the threes in the number 233,059,023?

   _____

Expanded Notation

CA Standard
KEY NS 1.1

Write 2,326,461 in expanded form.

Step **1** Write the number 2,326,461 in the place-value chart.

Millions				Thousands				Ones		
hundreds	tens	ones		hundreds	tens	ones		hundreds	tens	ones
		2	,	3	2	6	,	4	6	1

Step **2** Look at the digit on the far left of the chart. The value of the 2 is 2,000,000. Write this number with a plus sign. 2,000,000 +

Step **3** Continue through the chart from left to right, writing the value of each number with a plus sign. 300,000 + 20,000 + 6,000 + 400 + 60 + 1

Write the number in expanded form.

1. 1,452,580 _____

_____

2. 21,839,496 _____

_____

3. 313,407,203 _____

_____

4. 805,003,205 _____

_____

Spiral Review (Chapter 1, Lesson 2) NS 1.0

Write the value of the underlined digit.

5. 32,082,856 _____   **6.** 739,556,103 _____

7. Write four hundred six million, seven hundred twenty-two thousand, forty-one in standard form.

_____

Expanded Notation

CA Standard
KEY NS 1.1

Solve.

1. Write 2,215,450 in expanded form.

2. What is the correct way to write 3,000,000 + 800,000 + 70,000 + 5,000 + 100 + 20 + 5 in standard form?

3. What is the correct way to write 206,503,028 in expanded form?

4. What is the correct way to write 1,000 + 7,000,000 + 7 + 600,000,000 in standard form?

5. Henry wrote the expanded form of 55,400,000 as 55,000,000 + 400,000. Is he correct? Explain.

6. Which is greater 30,000,000 + 4,000,000 + 50,000 + 300 or 30,000,000 + 4,000,000 + 5,000 + 400? Explain.

Hands On: Compare and Order Whole Numbers

Compare 32,487 and 32,841.

Use a number line.

```
           32,487           32,841
    <----+----●---+----------●----+---->
  32,000       32,500            33,000
```

32,841 is to the right of 32,487 on the number line. So, 32,841 > 32,487.

Make a number line on a separate sheet of paper. Use > or < to compare the numbers.

1. 351 ◯ 531

2. 2,184 ◯ 1,284

3. 2,349 ◯ 7,439

4. 82,828 ◯ 88,222

5. 6,352 ◯ 6,325

6. 12,903 ◯ 19,902

7. 37,531 ◯ 37,135

8. 9,999 ◯ 11,026

9. 15,932 ◯ 15,942

Spiral Review (Grade 3 Chapter 17, Lesson 4) **KEY** NS 1.1

10. Use > or < to compare the numbers. 1.23 ◯ 0.13

11. Write these numbers in order from least to greatest. 3.24 4.02 3.44

_____

12. Jake has $34.82, Emily has $38.42, and Will has $34.28. Who has the most money? Who has the least?

_____

Hands On: Compare and Order Whole Numbers

CA Standard
KEY NS 1.2

Solve each problem.

1. The street where Jamie lives is 4,672 feet long, and the street where Eric lives is 8,193 feet long. Which street is shorter?

_____

_____

2. Jamie's class sold 1,862 tickets for the school raffle and Eric's class sold 2,139 tickets. Whose class sold more tickets?

_____

_____

3. Jamie's class went to Telescope Peak in Death Valley National Park on Wednesday and there were 1,049 visitors. Eric's class went on Friday, when there were 1,204 visitors. On which day did more people visit?

_____

4. In 2005, there were 827,775 visitors to Death Valley National Park. In 2004, there were 793,730, and in 2003, there were 924,182. Write the numbers of visitors in order from greatest to least.

_____

_____

5. The school bus drove up Telescope Peak to 8,133 feet above sea level. Then the students climbed further up on foot. Jamie climbed up to 8,689 feet. Eric climbed up to 8,722 feet. Who climbed higher?

_____

6. Nina is in Eric's class. She climbed up to 8,789 feet on Telescope Peak. Telescope Peak is 11,049 feet tall at its highest point. Write an expression using < or > to show the heights Nina, Jamie, and Eric climbed from least to greatest.

_____

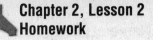
Compare and Order Whole Numbers Through Millions

CA Standards
KEY NS 1.2

Order 1,390,674 and 998,390 and 985,722 from least to greatest.

Line up the digits and find the greatest place where they differ.

1,390,674

 998,390

 985,722

The only number with a digit in the millions place is 1,390,674. It is the greatest number. The first place where the other two numbers differ is the ten thousands place: 8 < 9, so 985,722 < 998,390.

Solution: 985,722 < 998,390 < 1,390,674

Compare. Write > or < for each $\bigcirc$.

1. 298,942 $\bigcirc$ 289,942

2. 454,564 $\bigcirc$ 54,564

3. 567,195,753 $\bigcirc$ 576,195,753

4. 54,197,324 $\bigcirc$ 54,197,342

5. 3,748,573 $\bigcirc$ 3,747,326

6. 17,334,768 $\bigcirc$ 14,903,352

Spiral Review (Chapter 1, Lesson 4) **KEY** NS 1.1

7. Write 62,403,000 in expanded notation.

_____

8. Write 20 + 90,000 + 400 + 4,000 + 5,000,000 + 6 in standard form.

_____

9. The Marris family's warehouse contains 10 apples, 7,000 bananas, 20,000 plums, 300 oranges, and 100,000 grapes. Write the total number of pieces of fruit in standard form.

_____

Compare and Order Whole Numbers Through Millions

Solve each problem.

1. The Appalachian Trail is about 11,484,000 feet long. The Pacific Crest Trail is about 13,992,000 feet long. Which is longer?

   _____

   _____

2. The Continental Divide Trail is about 16,368,000 feet long. The American Discovery Trail is about 35,904,000 feet long. Which trail is shorter?

   _____

   _____

3. The North Country National Scenic Trail is about 24,288,000 feet long. Order the lengths of the North Country Trail, the Appalachian Trail, and the Pacific Crest trail from least to greatest.

   _____

   _____

   _____

4. Write the lengths of the North Country Trail, the American Discovery Trail, and the Pacific Crest Trail from greatest to least.

   _____

   _____

   _____

5. Maxine and Sam biked for six hours a day for five days. When they stopped, Sam had gone 2,376,827 feet, and Maxine had gone 2,376,791 feet. Who went farther?

   _____

6. Dexter was riding with Maxine and Sam. He rode for four hours and went 2,376,970 feet, but he took an extra break to fix his bike after he had gone 1,150,000 feet. List the numbers of feet Sam, Maxine, and Dexter rode from least to greatest.

   _____

   _____

   _____

Use with text pp. 28–30

Round Whole Numbers

CA Standard
KEY NS 1.3

Round the number 185,934 to the nearest thousand.

Find the place you want to round to.

185,936
↑
thousands place

The digit to its right is 5 or greater, so the digit in the rounded place increases.

185,934 rounds to 186,000.

Round each number to the place of the underlined digit.

1. 29,942

2. 842,049

3. 382,349

4. 879,923

_____ _____ _____ _____

5. 61,319

6. 56,932

7. 589,428

8. 258,299

_____ _____ _____ _____

Spiral Review (Chapter 2, Lesson 2) **KEY** NS 1.2, **KEY** NS 1.1

9. Write these numbers in order from greatest to least. 34,050   35,050   34,500

_____

10. Write these numbers in order from least to greatest.
690,172,349   699,074,213   69,010,342

_____

11. Joshua Tree National Park covers 789,866 acres. Yosemite National
Park covers 761,266 acres. Which park is larger?

_____

Round Whole Numbers

Solve each problem.

1. The tallest mountain in California is Mt. Whitney. It is 14,491 feet tall. Round its height to the nearest thousand.

   _____

2. David went bird watching and saw 17 birds. How many did he see, rounded to the nearest ten?

   _____

3. A park ranger told David he has seen 2,361 birds so far this year. About how many birds has the ranger seen, rounded to the nearest thousand?

   _____

4. Look at Problem 3. How many birds has the park ranger seen this year, rounded to the nearest hundred?

   _____

5. David asked the park ranger how old she was. She said, "When you round my age to the nearest 10, it's 30." What is the youngest age the ranger can be? What is the oldest?

   _____

6. Look at Problem 1. What is the height of Mt. Whitney, rounded to the nearest hundred? The nearest ten thousand?

   _____

More on Rounding Whole Numbers

CA Standard
KEY NS 1.3

Round the number 304,401,882 to the nearest million.

Underline the digit you are rounding to. Circle the digit to the right of it.

30<u>4</u>,④01,882

The circled digit is less than 5, so the underlined digit does not change. All the digits to the right of it change to 0.

Solution: 304,401,882 rounds to 304,000,000.

Round each number to the place of the underlined digit.

1. <u>3</u>,475,289

2. 103,<u>9</u>73,677

3. 7<u>0</u>,980,753

_____   _____   _____

4. 83<u>5</u>,900,672

5. 22,<u>2</u>99,409

6. 111,00<u>9</u>,485

_____   _____   _____

7. <u>4</u>8,007,878

8. 6<u>2</u>8,062,200

9. 5<u>2</u>,873,001

_____   _____   _____

Spiral Review   (Chapter 1, Lessons 2 and 3) **KEY** NS 1.1, NS 1.0

10. Write the number 209,399 in word form.

_____

_____

11. Write the number sixty-four thousand, four hundred two in standard form.

_____

12. Death Valley National Park covers 3,372,402 acres. What is the value of the 7 in that number?

_____

More on Rounding Whole Numbers

Solve each problem.

1. Point Reyes National Seashore has about 422,400 feet of coastline. How many feet is this, rounded to the nearest thousand?

_____

2. One cubic inch of beach sand can have about 125,000 grains of sand in it. Round the number of grains to the nearest ten thousand.

_____

3. The lighthouse at Point Reyes flashes once every five seconds, or 6,307,200 times in a year. About how many times does it flash in a year, rounded to the nearest hundred thousand?

_____

4. The lighthouse ran for 105 years, which means it probably flashed about 662,256,000 times. Round that number to the nearest ten million.

_____

5. There are 308 stairs in the lighthouse. The men who ran it had to go up about 9 times a day. They had to climb 2,772 steps a day and 1,011,780 steps a year. About how many steps did they go up in a year, rounded to the nearest hundred thousand?

_____

6. One man worked in the lighthouse for 24 years. He probably went up 24,282,720 steps. In the 105 years the lighthouse ran, the workers went up 106,236,900 steps. How many steps did the workers take in all, rounded to the nearest hundred million?

_____

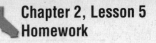

Problem Solving: Make an Organized List

CA Standards
MR 2.3, **KEY** NS 1.3

Burlington Elementary School had a general assembly at 10 A.M. on Tuesday. The assembly was attended by 116 first graders, 98 second graders, 162 third graders, and 139 fourth graders. About how many students attended the assembly altogether?

Step 1 Make a table of the important information in the problem.

Grade	Number of Students	Number of Students Rounded to Highest Place
1	116	100
2	98	100
3	162	200
4	139	100

Step 2 Round each number from the Number of Students column.

Solution: 100 + 100 + 200 + 100 = 500 students

Solve.

1. To the nearest *tenth*, about how many students attended the general assembly at Burlington Elementary? Complete the table to find the answer.

_____

Grade	Number of Students	Number of Students Rounded to Highest Place
1		
2		
3		
4		

Spiral Review (Chapter 1, Lessons 1 and 3) **KEY** NS 1.1

Write the number in standard form.

2. eight hundred ninety million, six hundred twenty-four thousand, one hundred six

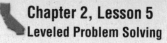
Problem Solving: Make an Organized List

CA Standards
MR 2.3, KEY NS 1.3

**Make an organized list to help you solve each problem.
Show your list.**

Tim's family is on vacation. On Monday they drove 276 miles. On Tuesday they drove 342 miles. The next day they drove 412 miles. The last day they drove 237 miles.

1. What day of the week was the last day of Tim's family's vacation?

_____

2. To the nearest ten, about how many miles did they drive on days that begin with *T* ?

_____

3. Put the days of the week in order according to the number of miles driven each day from least to greatest.

_____

_____

4. Put the number of miles driven each day in order from greatest to least.

_____

_____

5. To the nearest ten, about how many more miles did the family drive on Tuesday and Wednesday than on Monday and Thursday?

_____

6. How many more miles did the family drive on the last two days of their vacation than on the first two days?

_____

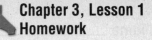
Hands On: Estimate and Check

CA Standard
KEY NS 3.0

Estimate 12 + 36 + 148.

Step 1 Round each addend to the nearest ten.

12 rounds to 10.

36 rounds to 40.

148 rounds to 150.

Step 2 Add the rounded numbers.

10 + 40 + 150 = 200

Solution: 12 + 36 + 148 is about 200.

Estimate the sum.

1. 62 + 51 + 94 = _____

2. 21 + 79 + 113 = _____

3. 226 + 95 + 134 = _____

4. 361 + 19 + 165 = _____

Spiral Review (Grade 3, Chapter 4, Lesson 5) **KEY** NS 1.3, NS 2.1

Estimate the sum or difference.

5. 152 − 98 = _____

6. 267 + 162 = _____

7. What is the difference between the sum of the two addends in problem 6 and the estimate of that sum?

_____

_____

Hands On: Estimate and Check

CA Standard
KEY NS 3.0

1. What is a close estimate of the sum of 8 + 17 + 34?

_____

2. What is a close estimate of the sum of 12 + 28 + 24?

_____

3. What is a close estimate of the sum of 18 + 141 + 88?

_____

4. What is a close estimate of the sum of 23 + 114 + 155?

_____

5. What is a close estimate of the sum of 139 + 177 + 208?

_____

6. What is a close estimate of the sum of 243 + 185 + 97?

_____

Addition Properties

CA Standards
KEY NS 3.1, AF 1.0

Complete the number sentence. $35 + 51 =$ _____ $+ 35$

Step 1 Look at the number sentence and decide which addition property could be used to help find the sum. This number sentence has two addends on each side of the equal sign. The addend 35 appears on both sides of the equal sign.

Step 2 The Commutative Property states that when you change the order of the addends the sum stays the same.

Step 3 Use the Commutative Property to identify the missing number.

Solution: $35 + 51 = \underline{51} + 35$

Copy and complete each number sentence. Tell which property of addition you used.

1. $(15 + 7) + 23 = 15 +$ _____

2. $542 + 0 =$ _____

3. $(27 + 18) + 13 = 27 +$ _____

4. $84 + 61 = 61 +$ _____

5. $0 + 753 =$ _____

Spiral Review   (Chapter 2, Lesson 3) **KEY** NS 1.3

Round each number to the place of the underlined digit.

6. $61,\underline{8}94$ _____

7. $82,\underline{5}93,071$ _____

8. Tanya counted 146 butterflies in a museum exhibit about insects. Rounded to the nearest ten, about how many butterflies did Tanya count?

_____

Addition Properties

CA Standards
KEY NS 3.1, AF 1.0

Find the number that makes each number sentence true. Tell which property of addition you used to find each answer.

1. Which number completes the number sentence ___ + 58 = 58?

   _____

   _____

2. Which number completes the number sentence $(9 + 1) + 49 = 9 + (1 + $___$)$?

   _____

   _____

3. Which number completes the number sentence 26 + 37 = ___ + 26?

   _____

   _____

4. Which number completes the number sentence 294 + 0 = ___?

   _____

   _____

5. Which number completes the number sentence $(18 + 52) + 28 = $___$ + (52 + 28)$?

   _____

   _____

6. Which number completes the number sentence 283 + 917 = 917 + ___?

   _____

   _____

Estimate Sums

CA Standards
KEY NS 1.3, **KEY** NS 3.0

Estimate 562 + 311.

Step 1 562 rounds to 600. 311 rounds to 300.

Step 2 Add the rounded numbers.
600 + 300 = 900

Solution: 562 + 311 is about 900.

Round each number to the nearest hundred. Then estimate the sum.

1. 722 + 236 =

_____

2.   3,229
       + 5,287

Round each number to the nearest ten. Then estimate the sum.

3.   942
       + 368

4. 951 + 513 =

_____

Round each number to the greatest place. Then estimate the sum.

5. 6,874 + 804 =

_____

6.   3,842
       + 690

Spiral Review (Chapter 2, Lesson 2) **KEY** NS 1.2

Compare. Write > or < for each ◯.

7. 4,392 ◯ 986

8. 625,860 ◯ 629,001

9. To attend a family reunion, Rachel traveled 892 miles, Daniel traveled 680 miles, and Stanley traveled 1,002 miles. Order the distances they traveled from least to greatest.

Estimate Sums

CA Standards
KEY NS 1.3, **KEY** NS 3.0

Estimate each sum by rounding numbers.

1. If you round to the nearest hundred, what is the sum of 622 + 285?

_____

2. If you round to the nearest ten, what is the sum of 349 + 61?

_____

3. If you round to the nearest hundred, what is the sum of 471 + 776?

_____

4. If you round to the nearest thousand, what is the sum of 1,839 + 733?

_____

5. If you round to the nearest thousand, what is the sum of 29,545 + 4,802?

_____

6. If you round to the nearest ten thousand, what is the sum of 36,439 + 17,882?

_____

Add Whole Numbers

CA Standards
KEY NS 3.1 KEY NS 3.0

Add 2,874 + 957.

```
  1 11
  2,874
+   957
  3,831
```

Regroup if the sum of the digits in a place value is 10 or greater.

Check by estimating.

```
  2,874 ⟶    3,000
+   957 ⟶ + 1,000
            4,000
```

3,831 is close to 4,000. The answer is reasonable.

Add. Use estimation to verify your answer.

1. 5,108
    + 4,843

2. 1,753
    + 4,637

3. 3,842
    + 3,584

4. 2,884
    + 4,067

5. 7,154 + 3,765 + 2,085 =

   _____

6. 5,324 + 5,841 + 8,935 =

   _____

7. 7,080 + 6,657 + 4,849 =

   _____

8. 9,084 + 6,743 + 8,654 =

   _____

Spiral Review   (Chapter 1, Lesson 2) **NS 1.0, KEY NS 1.1**

Write the value of the underlined digit.

9. 6̲21,087 _____

10. 3̲7̲9,458 _____

11. How would you write the number 38,872 in word form?

_____

_____

Add Whole Numbers

CA Standards
KEY NS 3.1, **KEY** NS 3.0

Add. Use estimation to verify your answers.

1. Remi has a collection of 189 glass marbles. Her brother, Taji, has 97 glass marbles. How many marbles do the two children have in all?

_____

2. Alberto and Alicia are putting colored beads into glass containers. Alicia counted 375 red beads, and Alberto counted 447 blue beads. How many beads did they count altogether?

_____

3. Public parks will be built on two plots of land. One park will cover 6,937 square feet of land. The second park will cover 3,505 square feet. How many square feet of land will these two new parks cover?

_____

4. A library received two donations of books to add to their collection. One donation consisted of 2,038 books. The second donation contained 773 books. If the library adds these books to its existing collection of 24,602 books, how many books will the library have in all?

_____

5. Devin did a word count in two large computer files. He found that the first file contained 512,694 words. The second file contained 388,790 words. If Devin puts the two files together, how many words will the new file have in all?

_____

6. Daniela was doing research on city populations in California. She learned that the state's Department of Finance published 2006 population estimates on its website. Daniela found the figure 411,755 for Oakland and the figure 210,158 for Fremont. If Daniela added these two numbers together, what would the combined population be?

_____

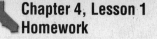
Hands On: Model Subtraction from 2,000

CA Standard
KEY NS 3.1

Mr. McFee had $2,000. He bought a used car for $840. How much money did he have left?

Step 1 Subtract $840 from $2,000. Represent $1,000 as ten $100 bills.

$| \longrightarrow$ |||||/||||

Step 2 Regroup one $100 bill as ten $10 bills.

$| \longrightarrow$
o o o o o
o o o o o

Step 3 Write a subtraction problem to show your final answer.

Solution: $2,000 − $840 = $1,160

Use play money to help you subtract.

1. $2,000 − $315 = _____

2. $2,000 − $86 = _____

3. $2,000 − $600 = _____

4. $2,000 − $892 = _____

5. $2,000 − $517 = _____

6. $2,000 − $276 = _____

Spiral Review (Chapter 3, Lesson 4) **KEY** NS 3.1

Add.

7. 506 + 492 = _____

8. 683 + 77 = _____

9. George had 108 bottle caps in his collection. Annie had 57 bottle caps. How many did they have together?

_____

Name _____ Date _____

Hands On: Model Subtraction from 2,000

CA Standard
KEY NS 3.1

Solve each problem.

1. The new department store sells 2,000 different items of clothing. It also sells 1,500 other products. How many more clothing items does the store sell?

   _____

2. Of the 2,000 clothing items, 750 are for men and the rest are for women. How many clothing items are for women?

   _____

3. The store was going to give prizes to its 2,000th customer. Lana was the 1,632nd customer. How many more people will walk into the store *before* the prize winner?

   _____

4. Jeff bought a new stove at the store for $795 plus a $30 delivery charge. He had $2,000 in his checking account before the purchase. After he wrote a check for the amount, how much money did he have left in his account?

   _____

5. Mr. Chee was interested in a new riding lawnmower that costs $2,000. He looked in his wallet and saw that he had a $500 bill, two $100 bills, a $50 bill and two $10 bills. How much more money does he need to buy the lawnmower?

   _____

6. The department store has 2,000 square feet of space inside. Of this space, 141 square feet are taken up by offices, 300 square feet by storage, and 75 by rest rooms. How much space remains for floor display space?

   _____

Name _____ Date _____

Estimate Differences

CA Standards
KEY NS 1.3, NS 2.1

Hector has $1,362. He buys a computer for $1,151. Does he have enough money left to buy an MP3 player for $160?

Step 1 Round each amount to the nearest hundred.

$1,362 rounds to $1,400.

$1,151 rounds to $1,200.

$$\begin{array}{r} 1,400 \\ -1,200 \\ \hline 200 \end{array}$$

Step 2 Compare the 2 numbers. Which is larger?

$200 > $160

Solution: Hector has enough money left to buy the MP3 player.

Round each number to the nearest hundred. Then estimate the difference.

1. $3,722 - 1,286 =$ **2.** $5,951 - 2,503 =$ **3.** $\$4,362 - \$1,764 =$ **4.** $55,229 - 23,287 =$

_____   _____   _____   _____

Round each number to the nearest thousand. Then estimate the difference.

5. $89,842 - 35,388 =$ **6.** $61,358 - 26,501 =$ **7.** $6,874 - 1,804 =$ **8.** $3,842 - 1,668 =$

_____   _____   _____   _____

Spiral Review (Chapter 2, Lessons 2 and 3) **KEY NS 1.2, NS 1.3**

Order from greatest to least.

9. 4,407,951   4,687,004   4,724,812

_____

10. 12,900,462   12,090,541   12,547,620

_____

11. What is 16,501 rounded to the nearest thousand?

_____

Estimate Differences

CA Standards
KEY NS 1.3, NS 2.1

Solve each problem.

1. The indoor sports arena seats 15,600 people. Last night's ball game was attended by 9,400 people. Round each number to the nearest thousand and estimate how many seats were empty at the game.

_____

2. The arena had a double header on Saturday. A total of 12,200 people attended the afternoon game and 13,900 came to the evening game. About how many more people attended the evening game? Round each number to the nearest thousand before finding the estimate.

_____

3. The stadium underwent minor renovations. It cost a total of $44,560. The stadium owners have paid the builder $20,942 so far. About how much money do they still owe for this work? Round to the nearest hundred and then estimate the difference.

_____

4. Receipts for the Friday night game were $80,522. Saturday's receipts were $94,268. About how much more money did the stadium take in on Saturday than Friday? Round to the nearest hundred and estimate.

_____

5. On Ladies' Day, a total of 4,566 women came to the stadium. There were 8,249 men and 1,522 children at the same game. About how many more men and children attended the game than women? Round each number to the nearest ten before estimating.

_____

6. Last season the stadium sold 23,921 cans of soda and 14,652 bottles of water to fans. They also sold 22,428 hot dogs and 13,756 hamburgers. About how many more beverages did they sell than sandwiches last season? Round each number to the nearest hundred before estimating.

_____

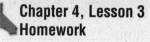
Subtract Whole Numbers

CA Standards
KEY NS 3.1, **KEY** NS 3.0

There are 3,745 students at Dan's school. 849 students bring their own lunch from home. How many students buy lunch in the school cafeteria?

Step 1 Subtract the ones.
$$\begin{array}{r} {\scriptstyle 3\ 15} \\ 3,7\cancel{4}\cancel{5} \\ -\ 8\ 4\ 9 \\ \hline 6 \end{array}$$

Step 2 Subtract the tens.
$$\begin{array}{r} {\scriptstyle 6\ 13\ 15} \\ 3,\cancel{7}\cancel{4}\cancel{5} \\ -\ 8\ 4\ 9 \\ \hline 9\ 6 \end{array}$$

Step 3 Subtract the hundreds and thousands.
$$\begin{array}{r} {\scriptstyle 2\ 16\ 13\ 15} \\ \cancel{3},\cancel{7}\cancel{4}\cancel{5} \\ -\ 8\ 4\ 9 \\ \hline 2,8\ 9\ 6 \end{array}$$

Solution: 2,896 students buy their lunch at the school cafeteria.

Subtract. Use addition or estimation to check.

1. 6,282 − 4,529 =   **2.** 8,510 − 2,238 =   **3.** 3,287 − 2,486 =   **4.** 9,125 − 5,306 =

_____   _____   _____   _____

Find each missing number.

5. _____ − 371 = 124   **6.** _____ + 5,495 = 7,621

7. 1,398 − _____ = 817

Spiral Review (Chapter 2, Lesson 3) **KEY** NS 1.3

Round each number to the nearest hundred thousand.

7. 11,256,893 _____   **8.** 3,832,999 _____

9. The state college has 6,892 male students and 8,439 female students. Round each number to the nearest thousand and then add to get an estimate of the total number of students.

_____

Subtract Whole Numbers

CA Standards
KEY NS 3.1, **KEY** NS 3.0

Solve each problem.

1. The botanical gardens have 1,246 plants native to the area and 767 exotic plants from other places. How many more plants are native than exotic?

2. Of the 767 exotic plants, 452 of them must live in greenhouses under controlled conditions. How many are grown out-doors?

3. A total of 2,854 people visited the botanical gardens last month. 1,986 have visited so far this month. How many more visitors must come before the month's end to match last month's attendance?

4. Of the 2,854 visitors last month, 892 were children and 761 were men. How many women visited the gardens?

5. Last year the botanical gardens had a total of 15,841 visitors. 8,602 of these visitors came during the summer months. Another 3,017 came in the fall. The gardens are closed in the winter. How many people came in the spring?

6. There are 1,262 red roses and 948 red tulips in the botanical gardens. There are 659 yellow daffodils and 1,107 white lilies. How many more red flowers are there than yellow and white flowers in the gardens?

Subtract Across Zeros

CA Standards
KEY NS 3.1, KEY NS 3.0

Subtract. 7,002 − 594

Step **1** Regroup one thousand as 10 hundreds.

$$\begin{array}{r} {}^{6}\ {}^{10}\\ \not{7},002 \\ -594 \end{array}$$

Step **2** Regroup one of hundreds as 10 tens.

$$\begin{array}{r} {}^{6}\ {}^{9}\ {}^{10}\ {}^{10}\\ \not{7},\not{0}\not{0}2 \\ -594 \end{array}$$

Step **3** Regroup one ten as 10 ones and subtract.

$$\begin{array}{r} {}^{6}\ {}^{9}\ {}^{9}\\ {}^{10}\ {}^{10}\ {}^{12}\\ \not{7},\not{0}\not{0}\not{2} \\ -594 \\ \hline 6,408 \end{array}$$

Solution: 7,002 − 594 = 6,408

Subtract. Estimate or add to check.

1. 4,000 − 335 =

2. 7,064 − 805 =

3. 3,080 − 1,064 =

4. 5,007 − 421 =

_____ _____ _____ _____

5. 7,004 − 2,840 =

6. 6,102 − 3,354 =

7. 5,320 − 2,299 =

_____ _____ _____

8. $60.00 − $56.85 =

9. $100.00 − $81.54 =

10. $50.00 − $28.74 =

_____ _____ _____

Spiral Review (Chapter 3, Lesson 2) **KEY NS 3.1**

Find the number that makes each number sentence true. Tell which property of addition you used.

11. 2,589 + 3,579 = 3,579 + ◯ _____

12. 0 + 10,986 = ◯ _____

13. Joyce rewrote (462 + 947) + 211 as 462 + (947 + 211). What property of addition was she using?

_____

Subtract Across Zeros

Solve each problem.

1. Harry has been collecting coins since he was 6. He has 700 coins in his collection. His father's coin collection has 1,040 coins. How many more coins does the father have than his son?

_____

2. Harry evaluated his coin collection to be worth $400. But a coin dealer offered to give him only $220 for it. Harry decided to keep his coins. What was the difference between his evaluation of his collection and the dealer's offer?

_____

3. Harry has 17 Indian head pennies and 53 Lincoln wheat-ear pennies in his collection. He also has 15 buffalo nickels and 47 older Jefferson nickels. How many more pennies does he have than nickels?

_____

4. Harry has 17 Indian head pennies and 53 Lincoln wheat-ear pennies in his collection. He also has 15 buffalo nickels and 47 older Jefferson nickels. Of the 700 coins in Harry's collection, how many are not pennies and nickels?

_____

5. Harry's dad gave him a silver dollar worth $20 and a Franklin half dollar worth $5.50 for his birthday. A friend offered Harry $40 for both coins. How much above the stated value would Harry get if he sold the coins?

_____

6. Harry visited a coin show. On display were 3,007 American coins and 1,526 foreign coins. How many more American coins than foreign coins were at the show?

_____

Name _____ Date _____

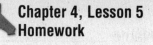

Chapter 4, Lesson 5
Homework

Problem Solving:
Too Much or Too Little Information

CA Standards
MR 1.1, KEY NS 3.1

Rachel took 60 pictures. It cost her $18 to develop the pictures. Anna took 12 fewer pictures than Rachael. How many pictures did Anna take?

What is the question?

• How many pictures did Anna take?

What do I need to know?

• How many pictures did Rachael take?

What do I know?

• Rachael took 60 pictures.
• Anna took 12 fewer pictures.

Solve the problem.

60 ← number of pictures Rachael took

−12 ← 12 fewer pictures

48 ← number of pictures that Anna took

Solution: Anna took 48 pictures.

Solve. If not enough information is given, tell what information is needed to solve the problem.

1. Billy recorded 6 songs for his new CD. Each song is about 4 minutes long. How much will Billy make if he sells 50 CDs?

_____

_____

2. Crystal is training to run a marathon. A marathon is about 26 miles. During the first three weeks of training, she will run 52 miles a week. During the next three weeks of training, she will run 60 miles a week. How many more miles will she run in week 5 than in week 2?

_____

Spiral Review (Chapter 3, Lesson 3) **KEY** NS 1.3, NS 2.1

Round each number to the nearest hundred. Then estimate the sum.

3. 427 + 872

_____ + _____ = _____

4. 5,789 + 7,246

_____ + _____ = _____

5. Jason counted his steps as he walked across the Golden Gate Bridge. He counted to 1,500 and stopped to rest. When he started to walk again, he started counting with 1 and counted 1,275 more steps. To the nearest hundred, about how many steps did Jason take as he walked across the bridge?

_____

Problem Solving: Too Much or Too Little Information

Use the information in the paragraph below to solve problems 1–4.

Problem Beverly sold tickets to the school play. She sold 28 tickets and collected $140. Jeff sold 15 tickets and collected $75. The tickets cost $5. How much more money did Beverly collect than Jeff?

1. What information do you need to solve the problem?

   _____

   _____

   _____

2. How will you solve the problem?

   _____

   _____

   _____

3. Do you have enough information to solve the problem? If so, solve and explain your steps. If not, what information do you need?

   _____

   _____

   _____

   _____

4. How can you tell if you have too much or too little information?

   _____

   _____

   _____

   _____

   _____

5. Eddie buys a box of 48 dog treats, 1 leash, and 2 bottles of dog shampoo for his puppy. Does Eddie have enough shampoo to give his puppy a bath every week for a month? Do you have too much or too little information to solve this problem?

   _____

6. Kylie put 4 dimes, 2 nickels, and 2 pennies in a bag. She and Samantha took turns pulling a coin from the bag until they each had 4 coins. How much money does each student have? Do you have too much or too little information to solve this problem?

   _____

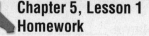
Hands On: Expressions with Parentheses

CA Standards
KEY AF 1.2, KEY AF 1.3

The answer to a problem can depend on what operation you do first.

$20 - 6 + 2 =$	$20 - 6 + 2 =$
$(20 - 6) + 2 =$	$20 - (6 + 2) =$
$14 + 2 = 16$	$20 - 8 = 12$

Always do the operation in parentheses first.

Add parentheses to make the value of the expression equal to 6.

1. $10 - 5 + 1$ 2. $14 - 5 + 3$ 3. $18 - 6 + 6$

Use the numbers to make an expression with a value of 30. Be sure to use +, −, and parentheses in each expression.

4. 48, 12, 6 _____

5. 28, 11, 13 _____

6. 85, 40, 15 _____

Spiral Review   (Chapter 3, Lessons 2 and 3) **KEY NS 1.3, AF 1.0.**

7. Round each number to the nearest ten thousand. Then estimate the sum.

$$23,789$$
$$+56,312$$

8. Find the number that makes the number sentence true. Tell what property of addition you used.

$186 + 59 = $ _____ $+ 186$

_____

_____

9. Round each number to the nearest thousand and estimate the sum.

$$48,926$$
$$+11,406$$

Hands On: Expressions with Parentheses

CA Standards
KEY AF 1.2, **KEY** AF 1.3

Solve each problem.

1. Which operation should you do *first* to get a value of 2 for $12 - 6 + 4$?

_____

2. Which operation should you do *first* to get a value of 8 for $20 - 13 + 1$?

_____

3. Which operation should you do *second* to get a value of 12 for $8 - 3 + 7$?

_____

4. Which operation should you do *second* to get a value of 3 for $14 - 5 + 6$?

_____

5. Use 30, 26, 18, 14, +, −, ( ), = to write an expression and its value.

_____

_____

6. Use 8, 18, 19, 45, +, −, ( ), = to write an expression and its value.

_____

_____

Write and Evaluate Expressions

CA Standards
KEY AF 1.2, AF 1.0

Simplify the expression $(30 - 5) + (12 - 7) - 3$.

Step 1 Do the operations in parentheses.
$$(30 - 5) + (12 - 7) - 3$$
$$25 \quad + \quad 5 \quad\quad -3$$

Step 2 Do the rest of the operations from left to right.
$$25 \quad + \quad 5 \quad\quad -3$$
$$30 \quad\quad\quad -3$$
$$27$$

Solution: $(30 - 5) + (12 - 7) - 3 = 27$

Simplify the expression.

1. $(62 - 7) - 9$

2. $(38 - 5) + 67$

3. $(8 + 16) + (37 + 17)$

_____

_____

_____

4. $(11 + 5) + (19 - 6)$

5. $(26 - 12) - (8 + 2)$

6. $(99 - 12) - (78 - 5)$

_____

_____

_____

Spiral Review (Chapter 3, Lesson 3) NS 1.4, **KEY** NS 2.1

Round each number to the nearest hundred. Then estimate the sum.

7. $412 + 189$

8. $3,850 + 1,218$

_____

_____

9. There are 5,580 gallons of water in one pond and 7,365 gallons of water in another pond. Round each number to the nearest thousand. Then estimate the total gallons of water in both ponds.

_____

Write and Evaluate Expressions

CA Standards
KEY AF 1.2, AF 1.0

Write and evaluate an expression to solve each problem.

1. Libby had 16 baskets of apples. She sold 12 baskets. Then she filled 8 more baskets. How many baskets of apples does she have now?

_____

_____

2. Joel saved $15 in May and $13 in June. Then he spent $20. How much money does Joel have now?

_____

_____

3. Viola made 45 "I ♥ Redwoods" T-shirts to sell at the fair. She sold 39 T-shirts. Then 3 people returned their shirts because they had "I ♥ Redwods" printed on them. How many shirts did Viola have left at the end of the day?

_____

_____

4. Richie found 12 marbles under his bed, 7 marbles on his desk, and 10 marbles on the floor of his closet. He put all the marbles in his pocket and 8 fell out of a hole. How many marbles does Richie have left?

_____

_____

5. Alani makes beaded bracelets. She had 86 round beads and 79 square beads. She used all but 9 of the round beads and all but 8 of the square beads. How many beads did Alani use?

_____

_____

6. Kenny blew up 95 red balloons. 26 of them broke. He blew up 31 blue balloons. 12 of them broke. He blew up 15 green balloons. None of them broke. How many blown-up balloons does Kenny have?

_____

_____

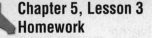
Expressions, Equations, and Inequalities

CA Standards
KEY AF 1.2, AF 1.0

When two expressions have the same value, you can write an **equation**.
You use = to show an equation.

$$(16 + 12) - 5 = 48 - (15 + 10)$$

When two expressions have different values, you can write an **inequality**.
You use < (is less than) or > (is more than) to show an inequality.

$$(31 + 9) - 6 > (17 - 6) + 22$$

$$(17 - 6) + 22 < (31 + 9) - 6$$

Write whether the number sentence is an equation or an inequality.

1. $60 - (48 \overset{44}{-} 4) = 16$

_____

2. $99 - (15 + 5) > (76 + 8) - 13$

_____

3. $(54 - 5) + 4 < 50 + 5$

_____

Spiral Review (Chapter 4, Lesson 2) **NS 2.1, KEY NS 1.3**

4. Round each number to the nearest thousand. Then estimate the difference.

$$\begin{array}{r} 80{,}754 \\ -12{,}136 \\ \hline \end{array}$$

5. Round each number to the nearest hundred. Then estimate the difference.

$$\begin{array}{r} 7{,}533 \\ -4{,}099 \\ \hline \end{array}$$

6. The population of Delano is 9,012 people. The population of Lakeport is 5,230 people. Round each number to the nearest thousand. Then estimate how much larger Delano's population is than Lakeport's population.

_____

Name _____ Date _____

Expressions, Equations, and Inequalities

CA Standards
KEY AF 1.2, AF 1.0

Use the data in the table to solve each problem. Use <, >, =, ( ) in your answer.

1. Write an inequality to compare the number of endangered birds and clams.

   _____

2. Write an inequality to compare the number of endangered fish and insects.

   _____

Endangered Species	
Group	**Number**
Clams	62
Birds	14 more than clams
Mammals	9 fewer than birds
Fish	70
Insects	half as many as fish
Reptiles	21 fewer than insects
Snails	10 more than reptiles

62
76
67
70
35
14
24

3. Write an inequality to compare the number of endangered insects and reptiles.

   _____

   _____

4. Write an inequality to compare the number of endangered reptiles and snails to the number of endangered mammals and insects.

   _____

   _____

5. Write an inequality to compare the number of endangered fish minus the number of endangered snails to the number of endangered clams minus the number of endangered insects.

   _____

   _____

6. Write an equation to compare the number of endangered mammals to 29 more than the number of endangered reptiles and snails.

   _____

   _____

Add Equals to Equals

You can add the same number to both sides of an equation.

Molly added 17 to both sides of this equation.

$$40 + 16 = 56$$

Is her new number sentence also an equation?

$$(40 + 16) + 17 \stackrel{?}{=} 56 + 17$$
$$73 = 73$$

Solution: Yes; $73 = 73$.

Complete.

1. $33 + 15 = 48$

$\bigcirc = 48$

2. $65 - 27 = \bigcirc$

$\bigcirc = \bigcirc$

3. $\bigcirc = 46 + 18$

$\bigcirc = \bigcirc$

4. $(58 - 31) + 14 = 27 + 14$

$\bigcirc + 14 = \bigcirc$

$\bigcirc = \bigcirc$

5. $16 + (31 + 42) = 12 + 77$

$16 + \bigcirc = \bigcirc$

$\bigcirc = \bigcirc$

6. $(74 - 21) + 37 = 55 + 35$

$\bigcirc + 37 = \bigcirc$

$\bigcirc = \bigcirc$

Spiral Review (Chapter 1, Lesson 4) **KEY NS 1.1**

7. Write 36,135 in expanded notation.

_____

_____

8. Write $400,000 + 90,000 + 9,000 + 500 + 20 + 3$ in standard form.

_____

9. The "Guess How Many Pennies" jar at the fair has 2,146 pennies.

Which digit is in the tens place?_____

Add Equals to Equals

Solve each problem.

1. Lilly and Evan are gathering money to spend at the fair. Lilly has saved $15 and she makes $12 raking the yard. Evan has saved $17 and gets $10 for his birthday. Write a mathematical sentence comparing the amount of money the children have to spend at the fair.

_____

_____

2. Lilly and Evan's mother gives each of the children an additional $5 to spend at the fair. Which child will have more money to spend at the fair?

_____

_____

3. Leroy has $27 to spend at the fair and Desmond has $25 to spend. Each of the boys buys a ticket to ride the roller coaster for $2. Write a mathematical sentence comparing the amount of money the boys have left.

_____

_____

4. A hamburger and a $2 drink cost $5.25. If potato chips cost $1.50, how much will a hamburger, a $2 drink, and potato chips cost? How do you know?

_____

_____

_____

5. If you know that $(47 - 13) + (85 + 17) = 136$, how can you find $(47 - 13) + (85 + 17) + 34$ quickly?

_____

_____

6. If you know that $(67 - 15) + 8 = 34 + (30 - 4)$, what number could you add to $(67 - 15) + 8$ to make it equal to $34 + (30 - 4) + (43 - 15)$?

_____

_____

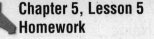
Problem Solving: Break a Problem into Parts

CA Standards
MR 1.2, **KEY** AF 1.3

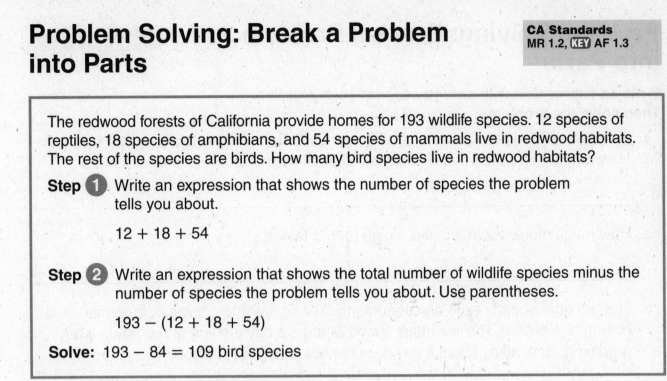

The redwood forests of California provide homes for 193 wildlife species. 12 species of reptiles, 18 species of amphibians, and 54 species of mammals live in redwood habitats. The rest of the species are birds. How many bird species live in redwood habitats?

Step 1 Write an expression that shows the number of species the problem tells you about.

12 + 18 + 54

Step 2 Write an expression that shows the total number of wildlife species minus the number of species the problem tells you about. Use parentheses.

193 − (12 + 18 + 54)

Solve: 193 − 84 = 109 bird species

Solve the problem by breaking it into parts. Write an expression that shows how to solve the problem.

1. Martin's birdwatching team counted 27 falcons, 9 owls, and 7 woodpeckers. Emma's team counted 17 falcons, 2 owls, and 8 woodpeckers. Which team counted more birds? How many more birds?

_____

_____

Spiral Review (Chapter 1, Lesson 4) **KEY** NS 1.1

Write the number in standard form.

2. 60,000 + 7,000 + 200 + 40 + 3

3. 500,000 + 80,000 + 500 + 80

_____   _____

4. When Casey wrote 3,208 in expanded form, he wrote 3,000 + 200 + 00 + 8. Is this correct? Explain your answer.

_____

Use with text pp. 104–105

Problem Solving: Break a Problem into Parts

CA Standards
MR 1.2, **KEY** AF 1.3

**Write an expression with parentheses for each problem.
Then solve the problem.**

1. A male Southern Sea Otter weighs 64 pounds. A female sea otter weighs 44 pounds. How much do 2 males and 3 females weigh altogether?

   _____

2. How much more would 3 males weigh than 3 females?

   _____

3. The sea otter spends each day performing 3 basic activities: feeding, grooming, and resting or sleeping. The sea otters spend 8 hours a day feeding and 5 hours a day grooming. How many hours a day does the sea otter rest or sleep?

   _____

Use the information in the table to answer problems 4 – 6. Write an expression with parentheses for each problem. Then solve the problem.

4. How many more adults and pups were counted in 1995 than in 1990?

   _____

   _____

Southern Sea Otter Census		
Year	Adults	Pups
1990	1,466	214
1995	2,095	282
2000	2,053	246

5. The Southern Sea Otter is threatened with extinction. According to the information on the table, did the population of sea otters increase or decrease between 1995 and 2000? Explain your answer.

   _____

   _____

6. The sea otter census is taken from the shore by two-person teams using binoculars and by two-person teams in airplanes flying over the ocean. If the shore teams in 1995 counted 1,007 adults and 152 pups, how many otters were counted by the airplane teams?

   _____

   _____

Hands On: Relate Multiplication and Division

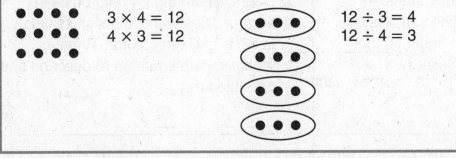

An **array** can show multiplication and division.

$3 \times 4 = 12$
$4 \times 3 = 12$

$12 \div 3 = 4$
$12 \div 4 = 3$

Write the multiplication and division equations for each array.

1.

2.

3.

_____
_____
_____
_____

_____
_____
_____

_____
_____

Spiral Review (Chapter 4, Lesson 3; Chapter 5, Lesson 2) **KEY** NS 3.0, **KEY** NS 3.1

4. Simplify the
   expression.

   $(25 + 13) + (46 - 10)$

   _____

5. Subtract.

   3,614
   − 1,509
   _____

6. Ursula gives Julio 23 of her Solar Adventures trading cards and 14 to Suri.
   If she started with 85 trading cards, how many does she have left?

   _____

Hands On: Relate Multiplication and Division

CA Standards
KEY NS 3.0, MR 2.3

Solve each problem.

1. Tranh has 18 dinosaur statues. He wants to arrange them in an array. Write a multiplication equation that describes one possible array.

_____

_____

2. Debra is planting 24 tulip bulbs in an array. She wants at least 3 bulbs in each row and column. Write a multiplication equation to describe one possible array.

_____

_____

3. Mac has 36 rocks in his collection. What are all the arrays he can make?

_____

_____

_____

4. María had her seashells in a 5×8 array. Then one shell broke. Write multiplication equations for all the arrays she can make using the new number of shells.

_____

_____

_____

5. Mr. Hansen has 48 pictures of his grandchildren. Write division equations to describe all the different arrays he can make with the pictures if he wants at least 3 pictures in each row.

_____

_____

_____

6. Sue has 50 stickers. She wants to arrange them in three different square arrays. Write multiplication equations to describe the arrays.

_____

_____

_____

Relate Multiplication and Division

CA Standard
KEY NS 3.0

Write the fact family for each array or set of numbers.

Some numbers can make a **fact family**. You can write multiplication and division equations using those numbers.

$3 \times 7 = 21$

$7 \times 3 = 21$

$21 \div 7 = 3$

$21 \div 3 = 7$

The numbers 3, 7, and 21 are a fact family.

1. ● ● ● ● ● ● ● ●
   ● ● ● ● ● ● ● ●

_____

_____

_____

_____

2. ■ ■ ■ ■ ■ ■ ■ ■
   ■ ■ ■ ■ ■ ■ ■ ■
   ■ ■ ■ ■ ■ ■ ■ ■
   ■ ■ ■ ■ ■ ■ ■ ■

_____

_____

_____

_____

3. 3, 5, 15

_____

_____

_____

_____

4. 4, 8, 32

_____

_____

_____

_____

5. 4, 7, 28

_____

_____

_____

_____

Spiral Review (Chapter 3, Lesson 4) **KEY** NS 3.1

Add. Use estimation to verify your answer.

6. $\begin{array}{r} 3,478 \\ +\ 655 \\ \hline \end{array}$

7. $\begin{array}{r} 17,961 \\ +\ 4,813 \\ \hline \end{array}$

8. Mrs. Fox traveled 338 miles from Chula Vista to Fresno and 295 miles from Fresno to Crescent City. How far did she travel in all?

_____

Relate Multiplication and Division

CA Standard
KEY NS 3.0

Use the numbers in each problem to write a fact family.

1. There are 36 buttons in 9 rows, with 4 buttons in each row.

   _____

   _____

   _____

2. Rusty planted 35 trees in 5 rows, with 7 trees in each row.

   _____

   _____

   _____

3. There are 4 rows, with 7 T-shirts in each row.

   _____

   _____

   _____

4. At Frank's Football Factory, there are 6 rows of footballs, with 8 balls in each row.

   _____

   _____

   _____

5. There are 63 stickers in 7 rows.

   _____

   _____

   _____

6. There are 56 candles in 8 rows on Mr. Booth's birthday cake.

   _____

   _____

   _____

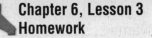
Multiplication Properties and Division Rules

CA Standards
KEY NS 3.0, AF 1.0

Use properties and rules to solve.

$1 \times 7 = \square$

The **Identity Property of Multiplication** states that when you multiply any number by one, the product is equal to that number.

Solution: $1 \times 7 = 7$

---

1. $6 \times 5 = 5 \times \square$

_____

2. $0 \times 61 =$

_____

3. $(3 \times 7) \times 2 = 3 \times (\square \times 2)$

_____

4. $1 \times 45 =$

_____

5. $0 \div 71 =$

_____

6. $\square \div 23 = 1$

_____

7. $29 \div \square = 29$

_____

Spiral Review (Chapter 5, Lessons 2–3) **KEY** AF 1.2, AF 1.0

8. Simplify the expression.
$(38 - 4) + 12$

_____

9. Complete the equation.
$20 + 7 = (16 - \square) + 14$

_____

10. Perry Porcupine has the sum of 73 and 15 quills. His sister Pamela has 7 fewer quills than Perry. Write an expression for the number of quills Pamela has.

_____

Multiplication Properties and Division Rules

CA Standards
KEY NS 3.0, AF 1.0

Solve each problem.

1. One billion is 1 followed by 9 zeros. What is 1 billion × 1?

   _____

2. One trillion is 1 followed by 12 zeros. What is 1 trillion × 0?

   _____

3. One quadrillion is 1 followed by 15 zeros. What is 1 quadrillion ÷ 1?

   _____

4. One quintillion is 1 followed by 18 zeros. What is 1 quintillion divided by 1 quintillion?

   _____

5. One septillion is 1 followed by 24 zeros. What is 0 ÷ 1 septillion?

   _____

6. One centillion is 1 followed by 303 zeros! What is 1 centillion divided by 0?

   _____

Name _____ Date _____

Hands On: Patterns in Multiplication and Division

CA Standards
KEY NS 3.0, MR 2.3

Multiplication

The product of two numbers is shown in the table in the square where the row and column of the two factors meet.

Division

To divide, find the column of the number you are dividing by. Look down the column to find the number you are dividing. Follow that row to the left to find the quotient.

columns

×	0	1	2	3	4	5	6	7	8	9
0	0	0	0	0	0	0	0	0	0	0
1	0	1	2	3	4	5	6	7	8	9
2	0	2	4	6	8	10	12	14	16	18
3	0	3	6	9	12	15	18	21	24	27
4	0	4	8	12	16	20	24	28	32	36
5	0	5	10	15	20	25	30	35	40	45
6	0	6	12	18	24	30	36	42	48	54
7	0	7	14	21	28	35	42	49	56	63
8	0	8	16	24	32	40	48	56	64	72
9	0	9	18	27	36	45	54	63	72	81

rows

Use the multiplication table to answer each question.

1. Find the product of 3 and 7 in two places in the table. Write two multiplication sentences using 3 and 7 as factors.

_____

2. Find the product of 5 and 9 in two places in the table. Write two multiplication sentences using 5 and 9 as factors.

_____

3. Find 42 in two places in the table. Write a division sentence for each 42.

_____

4. Find 36 in three places in the table. Write a division sentence for each 36.

_____

Spiral Review (Chapter 2, Lessons 3–4) **KEY NS 1.3**

Round each number to the place of the underlined digit.

5. 35,6̲71

_____

6. 842̲,105,367

_____

7. The Transamerica Pyramid in San Francisco is 10,236 inches high. How many inches is that rounded to the nearest thousand?

_____

Hands On: Patterns in Multiplication and Division

Use a multiplication table to solve.

1. Find the number 4 three times in the table. Write multiplication sentences and division sentences for each 4.

_____

_____

_____

2. Find the number 9 three times in the table. Write multiplication sentences and division sentences for each 9.

_____

_____

_____

3. Find the number 16 three times in the table. Write multiplication sentences and division sentences for each 16.

_____

_____

_____

4. Find the number 36 in the table. Write multiplication sentences and division sentences for each 36.

_____

_____

_____

5. Name five numbers that are found only once in the table.

_____

_____

6. What type of numbers is found an odd number of times in the table?

_____

_____

_____

Name _____ Date _____

Division with Remainders

Divide.

$21 \div 4$

$$\begin{array}{r} 5 \text{ R1} \\ 4\overline{)21} \\ -20 \leftarrow \text{Multiply. } 4 \times 5 \\ \hline 1 \leftarrow \text{Subtract. } 21 - 20 \\ \text{This is the remainder.} \end{array}$$

Solution: $21 \div 4 = 5$ R1

1. $5\overline{)29}$

2. $3\overline{)22}$

3. $7\overline{)31}$

4. $6\overline{)19}$

5. $15 \div 2 =$

6. $41 \div 7 =$

7. $52 \div 9 =$

_____

_____

_____

8. $35 \div 8 =$

9. $43 \div 5 =$

10. $28 \div 6 =$

_____

_____

_____

Spiral Review (Chapter 1, Lessons 2–3) **KEY** NS 1.1

11. Write the value of the underlined digit in 349,186.

_____

12. Write the number in standard form.
six hundred thirty-four thousand, one hundred twelve

_____

13. There were 238,754 visitors to the San Diego Zoo in one year.
Write the number in word form.

_____

_____

Division with Remainders

Solve each problem.

1. Callie had 38 stickers. She put 6 stickers on each of 6 pages. How many stickers were left over?

   _____

2. Aki has 99 buttons. She wants to put them on 11 sweaters equally, with no buttons left over. How many buttons will be on each sweater?

   _____

3. Kareem put 5 carrot sticks on each of 8 plates. He had 4 carrot sticks left over. How many carrot sticks does he have?

   _____

4. Lisa has 62 more pages to read in *Beezus and Ramona*. She plans to read 9 pages every night beginning on Monday. How many pages will she read on Sunday?

   _____

5. Josh has 2 dozen eggs. He uses 5 eggs for each extra-large loaf of his special pumpkin bread. How many loaves of bread can he bake? How many eggs will be left over?

   _____

6. Brendan has 75 stamps in his collection. He puts 8 stamps on each page in his album. How many more stamps does he need to fill 10 pages with no stamps left over?

   _____

Hands On: Expressions with All Four Operations

What is the value of $16 - 10 \div 2 \times 3$?

Step 1 Follow the order of operations. Evaluate $10 \div 2$ using number tiles.

| 1 6 | − | 5 | × | 3 |

Step 2 Now do the multiplication in the expression. Use the tiles to replace 5×3.

| 1 6 | − | 1 5 |

Step 3 Finish by doing the subtraction in the expression.
$16 - 15 = 1$

Solution: The value of $16 - 10 \div 2 \times 3$ is 1.

Use the numbers and operation symbols below to make an expression with the value of 6. Remember to follow the order of operations.

1. | 1 2 | 3 | 2 | × | − |

_____

2. | 1 4 | 1 6 | 2 | ÷ | − |

_____

3. | 2 | 2 | 2 | + | × |

_____

Spiral Review (Chapter 5, Lesson 3) **KEY** AF 1.2, AF 1.0

Use the numbers and symbols below to make each equation true .

4, 3, =, >

4. $8 - \square \times 2 \square\, 2$ _____

5. $10 - \square \div 2 \square\, 3$ _____

6. Molly has the equation $2 \times 3 + 6 - 5 = 13$. Where should she put parentheses to make this equation correct?

_____

Use with text pp. 142–143

Hands On: Expressions with All Four Operations

CA Standard
KEY AF 1.2, KEY AF 1.3

Solve each problem. Write an equation to get your answer. Remember that information from one problem will help you solve the next one.

1. John's family had an open house party on New Year's Day. 4 guests came at noon. Ten minutes later, 2 more guests arrived. At 12:30, one guest left. How many guests remained at the party?

_____

2. At 12:40, 6 more guests arrived at John's house. Then 2 couples left. How many guests are there now at the party?

_____

3. Over the next hour, the number of guests at the party tripled. Then, Mr. and Mrs. Ortiz and their three children left to go to another party. How many guests were left?

_____

4. By 2:30, half of the remaining guests had left. Then John's friends Gail, Bob, and Bob's cousin arrived and gave the party a needed lift. What was the guest count now?

_____

5. Bob and his cousin left at 4:15 and five minutes later John's Uncle Art, Aunt Louise, and their 4 children arrived, apologizing for being so late. Shortly after, 3 more couples left. How many guests are still at the party?

_____

6. After the other guests had gone, John's father invited Uncle Art and his family to stay for the night. They gratefully accepted. If John has two sisters besides his parents, how many people slept that night at his house?

_____

Expressions with All Four Operations

Evaluate $7 + (12 \div 3) \times 5$

Step 1 $7 + (12 \div 3) \times 5$ Simplify inside parentheses.

Step 2 $7 + 4 \times 5$ Multiply and divide from left to right.

Step 3 $7 + 20$ Add and subtract from left to right.

Solution: The value of $7 + (12 \div 3) \times 5$ is 27.

Simplify each expression. Follow the order of operations.

1. $(7 + 8) \times 2$

2. $(12 - 7) \times 8$

3. $(9 + 7) \div 8$

4. $25 + (4 \times 5) - 15$

5. $70 - (8 \times 5) \div 10$

6. $(28 - 4) \div 3$

Write an expression for each situation.

7. 38 fewer than 8 times 6 _____

8. 22 more than 25 divided by 5 _____

9. 159 fewer than 4 times the sum of 20 and 46 _____

Spiral Review   (Chapter 4, Lesson 3) **KEY** NS 3.1, **KEY** NS 3.0

10. Subtract. Use addition to check your answer.

     $5{,}291 - 3{,}682 =$ _____

11. Use inverse operations to find the missing number.

     $206 +$ _____ $= 389$

12. Ted had 500 bottle caps in his collection. Jan had 174 bottle caps in her collection. How many more bottle caps does Ted have than Jan?

_____

Expressions with All Four Operations

Write and evaluate an expression to solve each problem.

1. Hillary likes to take photographs with her camera. She took 40 pictures one week. She took twice as many the following week. How many pictures did she take in the two weeks?

_____

_____

2. Vic puts his photos in albums. He has 1 album of 25 pages. There are 4 photos on each page. He also has a 20-page album with 3 photos on each page. How many photos does he have in the two albums?

_____

_____

3. José took 3 rolls of film with him on the class field trip. Each rolls contains 36 pictures. He used up 2 rolls. There were 10 pictures left on the third roll when he got home. How many pictures of the class trip did José take?

_____

_____

4. Brad took the photos at his aunt's wedding. He took 22 pictures before the wedding, half as many during the wedding, and twice as many pictures after the wedding. How many wedding pictures did Brad take in all?

_____

_____

5. Lien went to the store to buy a new camera. The camera cost $86. She also bought 2 rolls of film that cost $5 each. She paid for her purchases with a $100 bill. What change did she receive back?

_____

6. Maria takes pictures in both black and white and color. She took 47 black and white pictures one day and 6 more than that in color. The same day, Teresa took 34 pictures in black and white and half as many in color. How many pictures did they both take that day?

_____

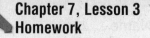
Equations and Inequalities with All Four Operations

CA Standard
AF 1.0

Ed read 9 books last summer. Angie read twice as many books as Ed. Hernando read 9 more books than Ed. In a number sentence, compare how many books Angie and Hernando read.

Step 1 Write an expression for the number of books each person read.

Books read by Angie	Books read by Hernando
9×2	$9 + 9$

Step 2 Evaluate each.

9×2	$9 + 9$
18	18

Step 3 Compare the 2 evaluations.

9×2	$=$	$9 + 9$
18	$=$	18

Solution: $9 \times 2 = 9 + 9$

Copy and complete. Use >, <, or =.

1. $(100 - 40) \times 2 \bigcirc 100 + 20$

2. $20 + (2 \times 3) \bigcirc 30 \div 2$

3. $8 + 7 \bigcirc 1 \times 15$

4. $(6 \times 8) + 10 \bigcirc \frac{40}{10} \times (5 \times 10)$

5. $15 - (6 \times 2) \bigcirc (16 \div 4) + 1$

6. $(70 \div 2) + 5 \bigcirc (2 \times 15) + 10$

Spiral Review (Chapter 5, Lesson 4) **KEY AF 1.2, KEY AF 2.0**

Copy and complete.

7. $34 - 16 = 18$

_____ $= 18$

8. $(86 + 12) - 31 = 34 + 33$

_____ $- 31 =$ _____

_____ $=$ _____

9. What do you know about the value of the $\bigcirc$ and $\triangle$ in this equation?

$\bigcirc \times 6 = \triangle \times 6$ _____

Use with text pp. 148–150

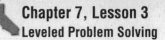
Equations and Inequalities with All Four Operations

CA Standard
AF 1.0

Write equations or inequalities to solve the problems.

1. Bill went on 4 rides at the amusement park. Juanita went on twice as many rides as Bill did. Henry went on 4 more rides than Bill did. Compare how many rides Juanita went on to how many rides Henry went on.

_____

2. Each ride at the amusement park requires tickets. The merry-go-round costs 2 tickets. The Ferris wheel costs 2 times as many tickets. The roller coaster costs 4 more tickets than the merry-go-round. Compare how many tickets needed to ride the Ferris wheel to the number needed to ride the roller coaster.

_____

3. The shooting gallery on the midway awarded 40 stuffed animals as prizes one week. The ring toss awarded 30 more stuffed animals than the shooting gallery. The softball throw presented patrons with twice as many stuffed animals than the shooting gallery. Compare the number of stuffed animals given by the ring toss to the number given by the softball throw.

_____

4. The concession booth sold 75 cotton candies one night at the amusement park. It also sold 3 times as many cups of lemonade. People bought 70 more bags of popcorn as they did cotton candies. Compare the number of cups of lemonade sold that evening to the number of bags of popcorn sold.

_____

5. One night 350 people visited the park's haunted house. Half as many attended the magic show. 100 fewer people attended the fun house as the haunted house. Compare the number who attended the magic show to the number who went into the fun house.

_____

6. A total of 650 people came to the amusement park on Thursday night. 456 more admissions were recorded on Friday night. Three times as many patrons went to the park on Saturday night as on Thursday night. Compare the number of paid admissions on Friday night to those on Saturday night.

_____

Multipy Equals by Equals

CA Standards
KEY AF 2.2, KEY AF 2.0

Will the equation $3 \times 6 = 2 \times 9$ still be true if both sides are multiplied by 5?

Step 1 Simplify both sides of the equation.

$3 \times 6 = 2 \times 9$
$18 \quad = 18$

Step 2 Rewrite the equation multiplying each side by 5.

$18 \times 5 = 18 \times 5$

$90 \quad = \quad 90$

Step 3 Note that both sides are equal as they were before.

Solution: The equation $3 \times 6 = 2 \times 9$ remains true if both sides are multiplied by 5.

Copy and complete.

1. $5 \times (2 + 1) = 5 \times$ _____

2. $(6 - 2) \times$ _____ $= 4 \times 9$

3. $4 + (9 - 2) = 4 +$ _____

4. $12 \times 2 + 5 = 12 + 12 +$ _____

5. $(8 \div$ _____$) \times 3 = 4 \times 3$

6. _____ $+ (6 \times 7) = 8 + 42$

7. $4 \times ($_____$ + 2) = 4 \times 8$

8. $7 \times (20 \div 5) = 7 \times$ _____

Spiral Review (Chapter 6, Lesson 4) **KEY** NS 3.0, MR 2.3

9. Divide. Then check your answer.

   $18 \div 6 =$ _____

10. Find the missing number.

    $21 \div$ _____ $= 3$

11. Jake has 15 apples. He gave one third of the apples to Judy. How many apples did he give her?

    _____

Use with text pp. 152–153

Multiply Equals by Equals

Solve each problem. After the answer write an equation that helped you to get the answer.

1. Alex picked 8 apples and 2 pears from the orchard. Janet picked 4 apples. How many pears does she have to pick to have the same amount of fruit as Alex?

_____

2. Jorge filled 2 bags with 4 peaches in each bag. Rod has only one bag. How many peaches must he put in his bag to equal Jorge's number of peaches?

_____

3. A farmer had six baskets of pears. Each basket held 15 pears. He lost one of the baskets when it fell off his tractor. How many pears does he now have?

_____

4. Hector has 3 apple trees in his yard. Each tree has 50 apples. Jill has 5 apple trees in her yard. How many apples must each tree in Jill's yard have to match the number of apples Hector has?

_____

5. Ling bought 8 oranges and ate 2 of them. Carl bought twice as many oranges as Ling. How many oranges must he eat to have the same number of oranges as Ling?

_____

6. Ben picked 6 baskets of avocados. Each basket held 30 avocados. 40 avocados were bad and had to be thrown away. Thad picked 5 baskets and 10 were bad. He had the same number of avocados as Ben. How many avocados did he have in each basket?

_____

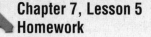
Problem Solving:
Write an Expression

Write an expression to solve each problem.

Read It Look for information.

Mr. Henderson bought 5 cups and 5 saucers. His total purchase cost $50.
If each saucer cost $2, how much did he pay for each cup?

Organize It Write an expression to solve the problem.

| ($50 | − | 5 × $2) | ÷ | | 5 | = | _____ |

total
purchase

cost of
saucers

number
of cups

cost of each cup

Solve It First, do the operations inside the parentheses. Do the multiplication and division in order from left to right. Then, do the addition and subtraction in order from left to right. Finally, do the operations outside the parentheses in the same order.

Each cup cost _____

---

1. Mrs. Henderson bought 18 pieces of pottery. She bought 11 mugs, 4 bowls, and some plates. How many plates did she buy?

_____

2. She also bought 3 hand mirrors, 2 spoon rests, and 5 toothbrush holders to give as gifts to her friends. The hand mirrors cost $5 each. The spoon rests cost $2 each. Altogether, she spent $34 on the gifts. How much did the 5 toothbrush holders cost?

_____

Spiral Review (Chapter 6, Lesson 5) **KEY** NS 3.2

Divide. Then check your answer.

3. 17 ÷ 3 = _____   **4.** 126 ÷ 10 = _____

5. Margie wants to ship 40 mugs. Each shipping carton holds 12 mugs. How many full cartons will she have? How many mugs will be left over?

_____

Problem Solving:
Write an Expression

Write an equation to solve each problem.

1. Mandy has 9 coins. The coins are quarters, dimes, and nickels. She has 2 quarters and 5 nickels. How many dimes does Mandy have?

_____

2. Annie has 16 coins. The value of the coins totals 50 cents. She has 10 pennies and 2 dimes. The rest of the coins are nickels. How many nickels does she have?

_____

3. Mandy has $37. She has 2 one-dollar bills and 1 ten-dollar bill. The rest are five-dollar bills. How many five-dollar bills does she have?

_____

_____

_____

4. Annie had $38. She bought 3 CDs and a book. She had $4 left over. If the CDs cost $9 each, what did the book cost?

_____

_____

5. Teri bought 3 T-shirts and 2 pairs of socks. She paid a total of $30. If the socks were $3 a pair, how much was each T-shirt?

_____

_____

6. Meredith bought 4 notebooks that cost $2 a piece. She also bought 3 packs of pencils for $6 total. She had a $3 off coupon for purchases of $10 or more. How much did she spend on school supplies?

_____

_____

Hands On: Variables

CA Standards
AF 1.0, AF 1.1

Evaluate $3n + 2$ when $n = 4$. Think: What would be the value of the same expression if n had a value of 4?	Replace n with 4. The expression now becomes $3 \times 4 + 2$, or $12 + 2$, which is equal to 14.	Solution: When $n = 4$, $3n + 2$ equals 14.

Evaluate each expression.

1. $(n + 2) \times 10$ when $n = 5$ _____

2. $(4 \times p) + (5 \times p)$ when $p = 3$ _____

3. $(7 \times k) - 2$ when $k = 4$ _____

4. $r + 10$ when $r = 5$ _____

5. $16 \div a$ when $a = 4$ _____

6. $(n + 2) \times (n - 2)$ when $n = 2$ _____

7. $15 + (3 \times e)$ when $e = 0$ _____

8. $f + (2 \times f)$ when $f = 1$ _____

Spiral Review (Chapter 7, Lesson 2) **AF 1.2**

Simplify each expression.

9. $4 \times (3 + 5)$ _____

10. $(5 + 4) + (6 - 2)$ _____

11. A class consists of 3 groups of 5 students and 2 groups of 4 students. How many students are in the class?

_____

Hands On: Variables

Solve.

1. Kenny has 3 more apples than Jenny. If Jenny has *j* apples, write an expression to how many apples Kenny has.

   _____

2. Basha studied for 2 fewer hours than Sonja did. If Sonja studied for *s* hours, how many hours did Basha study?

   _____

3. A square has four equal sides. If the perimeter (sum of all of the sides) of the square is *p*, what is the length of each side?

   _____

4. The perimeter of a triangle is *c* inches. If each side is the same length, what is an algebraic expression for the length of each side?

   _____

5. If sweaters sell for *s* dollars each and T-shirts sell for *t* dollars each, what is an algebraic expression for the cost (in dollars) of 7 sweaters and 5 T-shirts.

   _____

6. Mateo is counting his change. If he has *q* quarters and *d* dimes, what is an algebraic expression representing the total amount of change (in cents) in his pocket?

   _____

Write and Evaluate Algebraic Expressions

CA Standards
AF 1.0, AF 1.1

If Martha bakes p pies and Cindy bakes 5 times as many pies as Martha, write an expression for the number of pies Cindy bakes.	If $p = 40$, how many pies does Cindy bake?
Since Cindy bakes 5 times as many pies as Martha, multiply the number of pies Martha bakes by 5.	Use the expression $5p$ and replace p with 40.
Solution: The correct expression is $5p$.	$5p$ 5×40 200 **Solution:** Cindy bakes 200 pies.

Write an expression that matches the words.

1. 10 less than the number of ducks

_____

2. 5 times the number of penguins

_____

3. 4 more than twice the number of geese

_____

4. 5 less than three times the number of chipmunks

_____

Evaluate each expression when $n = 2$.

5. $4n + 4 =$ _____

6. $5 \times (n - 1) =$ _____

7. $8 + 9n =$ _____

8. $(n + 2) \times (n + 10) =$ _____

Spiral Review (Chapter 5, Lesson 2) **AF 1.0**

Write an expression for the situation.

9. 17 fewer than 44 _____

10. 100 more than the difference between 88 and 66 _____

11. Joshua has 3 quarters. Alex has 10 more than 2 times as many quarters as Joshua. Write an expression for how many quarters Alex has. Evaluate the expression.

_____

Write and Evaluate Algebraic Expressions

CA Standards
AF 1.0, AF 1.1

Solve.

1. Eric scored 14 points higher than Caelin on a math quiz. Write an expression that shows Eric's score if Caelin's score is *s*.

_____

2. Using the expression you wrote in problem 1, what would Eric's score be if Caelin's score is 80?

_____

3. Max has 5 more than twice as many cookies as Chris. Write an expression that shows the number of cookies Max has if Chris has *c* cookies.

_____

4. Using the expression you wrote in problem 3, how many cookies does Max have if Chris has 12 cookies?

_____

5. Emma sees *m* movies in 3 weeks. What is an expression for the number of movies Emma sees in 12 weeks?

_____

6. Analee earns $45 for every 5 hours of work. How much money can she earn for *h* hours of work?

_____

Solve Addition and Subtraction Equations

CA Standards
KEY AF 2.0, **KEY** AF 2.1

Solve the equation.	Check the solution.
$w + 10 = 15$	$w + 10 = 15$
Use inverse operations.	$5 + 10 = 15$
$w + 10 = 15$	$15 = 15$ ✓
$w + 10 - 10 = 15 - 10$	
$w = 5$	
Solution: $w = 5$	

Solve the equation. Check the solution.

1. $4 + y = 10$ _____

2. $k - 4 = 6$ _____

3. $m + 16 = 40$ _____

4. $2 + j = 100$ _____

5. $e + 33 = 44$ _____

6. $r - 200 = 300$ _____

7. $b - 24 = 56$ _____

8. $89 + q = 100$ _____

Spiral Review (Chapter 6, Lesson 4) **KEY** NS 3.0, MR 2.3

Use a multiplication table for the following problems.

9. How many times does 12 appear on the multiplication table?

_____

10. What are the factors of 12?

_____

11. Write the square numbers between 1 and 40. Describe the pattern the square numbers make on the multiplication table.

_____

_____

Solve Addition and Subtraction Equations

CA Standards
KEY AF 2.0, KEY AF 2.1

Solve.

1. Timani has 3 more boxes than Trevor. If Timani has 17 boxes, write and solve an equation to show how many boxes Trevor has.

_____

2. Paul and Steve ate a box of 7 cupcakes. Steve ate 4 cupcakes. Paul ate the rest. How many cupcakes did Paul eat?

_____

3. Manuel painted 4 houses over the summer. John painted x houses. Patrick painted 2 houses. They painted 9 houses in all. How many houses did John paint?

_____

4. Sarah is x inches taller than Roberta, who is 60 inches tall. Together they are 130 inches tall. How much taller is Sarah than Roberta?

_____

5. A deck of 52 cards is distributed to 4 students. Rob gets 10 cards, Mike gets 12 cards, Mary gets 14 cards and Linda gets the rest. How many cards does Linda get?

_____

6. If a is 5 less than b, b is 2 more than c and c is 3 less than d, how much more or less is a than d?

_____

Solve Multiplication and Division Equations

CA Standards
KEY AF 2.0, KEY AF 2.2

Solve the equation.	Use inverse operations.	Check:
$5a = 15$	$5a = 15$ $5a \div 5 = 15 \div 5$ $a = 3$ **Solution:** So, $a = 3$.	$5a = 15$ $5 \times 3 = 15$ $15 = 15\ \checkmark$

Solve the equation. Check the solution.

1. $2y = 10$ _____

2. $5x = 25$ _____

3. $a \div 7 = 20$ _____

4. $6b = 42$ _____

5. $c \div 3 = 15$ _____

6. $40p = 800$ _____

7. $d \div 2 = 8$ _____

8. $11q = 121$ _____

Spiral Review (Chapter 7, Lesson 2) **KEY** AF 1.2, **KEY** AF 1.3

Evaluate the expressions below.

9. $(3 \times 12) + 3 \times 8$ _____

10. $3 + 9 \times 3 - 8 \times 2$ _____

11. Adriana says $3 + 2 \times 3 = 15$. Deborah says $3 + 2 \times 3 = 9$.
Which student is correct? Why?

_____

_____

Solve Multiplication and Division Equations

CA Standards
KEY AF 2.0, KEY AF 2.2

Solve.

1. Rhonda bakes *p* pies. Mary bakes 3*p* pies. If together they bake 20 pies, how many pies does Mary bake?

   _____

2. Ralph bought 4 books for *k* dollars each. Iris bought 5 books for *k* dollars each. If together they spend 90 dollars, how much is each book?

   _____

3. Ben read *b* books. Kirsten read 2*b* books. If together they read 30 books, how many books did Ben read?

   _____

4. Laura is 2 inches taller than Rebecca. Maxine is 4 inches taller than Rebecca. The total height for the three girls is 150 inches. How tall is Rebecca?

   _____

5. The sum of three consecutive numbers (one after the other) is 12. What is the smallest number?

   _____

6. Gibby has 3 more pencils than Allie. Lina has 2 times as many pencils as Allie. Together, Gibby, Lina and Allie have 15 pencils. How many pencils does Allie have?

   _____

Problem Solving: Use Equations for Comparison Problems

CA Standards
MR 2.3, **KEY** AF 2.0

Asian lions are an endangered species. There are only 460 Asian lions known to exist. Researchers have counted 260 Asian lions in the wild on a reserve in India that used to be royal hunting grounds. The other Asian lions are in zoos around the world. How many Asian lions are in zoos?

Step 1 Write an equation using the total number of Asian lions and the number of Asian lions in India. Let x represent the number of lions in zoos.

$260 + x = 460$

Step 2 Use an inverse operation to find the value of the variable.

$260 + x - 260 = 460 - 260$

Solve: $x = 200$ Asian lions in zoos

Write an equation to solve. Use x to represent the unknown amount.

1. A female leopard weighs 132 pounds. A male leopard weighs 200 pounds. How much more does a male leopard weigh than a female leopard?

   _____

2. A leopard's top speed is 35 miles per hour. A cheetah can run twice as fast as a leopard. How fast can a cheetah run?

   _____

Spiral Review (Chapter 7, Lesson 3) **AF 1.0**

Complete using >, <, or =.

3. $(4 + 7) \times 3$ ____ $4 + 7 \times 3$

4. $14 + (2 \times 5) - 8$ ____ $(8 \times 8) \div 8$

5. Alex saw 6 lions. Mark saw 3 times the number of lions that Alex did. Jeff saw 12 more lions that Alex. Write a number sentence that compares how many lions Mark saw to how many Jeff saw.

   _____

   _____

Problem Solving: Use Equations for Comparison Problems

CA Standards
MR 2.3, **KEY** AF 2.0

Write an equation to solve each problem. Use *a* as the variable in each equation. Solve the equation.

1. During the last thirty years, Best in Show at the Westminster Kennel Dog Show has been won by terriers at 8 shows and by spaniels at 5 shows. At how many more shows have terriers won than spaniels?

   _____

2. Mrs. James Edward Clark has been a judge at 23 Westminster Dog Shows. J. D. Jones has been a judge at 2 shows. How many more shows has Mrs. Clark judged than Mr. Jones?

   _____

3. Since 1930, Norwegian elkhounds have won in the Hound Group 3 times more often than basset hounds. Norwegian elkhounds have won the Hound Group in 15 shows. In how many shows have basset hounds won the Hound Group?

   _____

4. Best of Group in the Toy Group often goes to Pekingeses, toy poodles, and Pomeranians. Since 1924, the award has gone to a toy poodle at 10 shows. A Yorkshire terrier has received the award only half that many times. At how many shows has the toy Group award gone to a Yorkshire terrier?

   _____

5. The first Westminster Dog Show was held in 1877. There were 1,177 dogs entered in the show. One hundred years later, in 1977 there were 2,624 dogs entered in the show. Today there is a limit of 2,500 dogs. How many more dogs were entered in the 1977 show than in the 1877 show?

   _____

6. For the first hundred years of the show, it was held in Gilmore's Garden 3 years, in the American Institute 3 years, and in the New Grand Central Palace 4 years. The show was at a location called Madison Square Garden all the *other* years. During the first hundred years, how many times was the show held in Madison Square Garden?

   _____

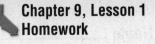
Hands On: Function Tables

CA Standards
KEY AF 1.5, MR 1.1

Copy and complete the function table by continuing the pattern.

The Marshall family is hosting a barbecue. Mr. Marshall is cooking two dozen ears of corn. Mr. Marshall has planned for each person to eat 2 ears of corn. How many ears of corn will be eaten by Mr. and Mrs. Marshall?

Number of People	Number of Ears Served
1	2
2	4
3	
5	
9	

Step ❶ Read the question and look carefully at the function table. Write the number of ears one person will eat in the first row of the right column. Identify the function rule of the table. To complete this table, you will need to multiply each number of people by 2.

Step ❷ Fill in the second row by continuing the pattern. $2 \times 2 = 4$

Step ❸ Fill in the remaining rows using the same pattern.

Solution: Mr. and Mrs. Marshall will eat 4 ears of corn.

1. How many ears of corn will be eaten by a family of 3? _____

2. How many ears of corn will be eaten at a table of 5 guests? _____

3. How many ears will be left over if there are a total of 9 people at the barbecue? ____

Spiral Review   (Chapter 8, Lesson 2) **AF 1.1**

Solve each expression for $x = 3$.

4. $2x + 8$ _____

5. $4x + 5$ _____

6. What value must you identify to solve for j in the equation $j = 4k - 4$?

_____

Hands On: Function Tables

CA Standards
KEY AF 1.5, MR 1.1

Use the function tables to answer the following questions.

There are 4 pens in each package.

Number of Packages	Number of Pens
1	4
2	
3	

1. How many pens are there in 2 packages? _____

2. How many pens are there in 3 packages? _____

There are 6 windows in each room.

Number of Rooms	Number of Windows
1	6
2	
4	

3. How many windows are there in 2 rooms? _____

4. How many windows are there in 4 rooms? _____

There are 14 desks in each classroom.

Number of Classrooms	Number of Desks
1	14
3	
5	

5. How many desks are there in 3 classrooms? _____

6. How many desks are there in 5 classrooms? _____

Write Function Rules Using One Variable

CA Standards
KEY AF 1.5, AF 1.1

Complete the function table.

Rule: Output = 3x

Input (x)	Output
1	3
2	6
3	9

Step 1 Look at the function table, and read the function rule carefully. In this function rule and function table, the variable is x.

Step 2 See how the function rule applies in the chart. In the first row, the input is 1. Because of the function rule, multiply 1 × 3 to find an output value of 3. In the second row, the input is 2. To apply the function rule, multiply 2 × 3 to find an output value of 6.

Step 3 Apply the function rule to the input value of 3.
$3 \times 3 = 9$

Solution: The output value is 9.

Rule: Output = 4t + 5

Input (t)	Output
2	
4	
6	

1. What is the output value if the input value is 2? _____

2. What is the output value if the input value is 4? _____

3. What is the output value if the input value is 6? _____

Spiral Review (Chapter 7, Lesson 4) **KEY AF 2.0, KEY AF 2.2**

Complete.

4. $4 \times (12 - 7) =$ _____ $\times 5$

5. $8 \times (28 \div 4) = 8 \times$ _____

6. What do you know about the value of the △ and the ☆ in this equation?

$$\triangle \times 11 = 11 \times \star$$

_____

_____

_____

Name _____ Date _____

Write Function Rules Using One Variable

CA Standards
KEY AF 1.5, AF 1.1

Use the function table to answer the following questions.

Input (y)	Output
2	
3	
5	
8	

1. If the rule is Output = $y + 7$, what is the output value when $y = 2$? _____

2. If the rule is Output = $y + 7$, what is the output value when $y = 5$? _____

3. If the rule is Output = $25 - 3y$, what is the output value when $y = 3$? _____

4. If the rule is Output = $25 - 3y$, what is the output value when $y = 8$? _____

5. If the rule is Output = $(9 + 3y) \div 2$, what is the output value when $y = 3$? _____

6. If the rule is Output = $(9 + 3y) \div 2$, what is the output value when $y = 5$? _____

Use with text pp. 192–194

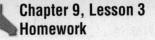

Write Function Rules Using Two Variables

Compete each function table or rule.

Rule: $t = 4s$	
Input (s)	Output (t)
5	20
6	24

← 5 × 4
← 6 × 4

Step 1 Look at the function rule and the function table carefully. Note that s stands for the input, and t stands for the output. The rule shows that the input multiplied with 4 equals the output.

Step 2 The first row of the table gives an input value of 5. Since 5 × 4 = 20, the output value is 20.

Step 3 To find the output value when the input value is 6, replace the variable s with 6 and multiply.

6 × 4 = 24

Solution: When the input value is 6, the output value is 24.

	Rule: $b = a + 7$	
	Input (a)	Output (b)
1.	7	
2.	11	
3.	15	

	Rule: $y = 3x$	
	Input (x)	Output (y)
4.	4	
5.	6	
6.		6

7.	Rule: _____	
	Input (x)	Output (y)
	27	9
	30	10
	45	15

Spiral Review (Chapter 8, Lesson 2) AF 1.1, AF 1.0

Evaluate each expression when $v = 6$.

8. $12v$ _____

9. $8 + 3v$ _____

10. Paula and Julia walk to school. Paula walks half as far as Julia. How far does Julia walk? Write an equation using two variables for this problem.

_____

Write Function Rules Using Two Variables

CA Standards
KEY AF 1.5, AF 1.1

Use each function table to answer the pair of questions that follows.

Rule: $c = 3 + 5b$

Input (b)	Output (c)
2	
5	

1. What is the output value if the input value is 2? _____

2. What is the output value if the input value is 5? _____

Rule: $t = 6s - 4$

Input (s)	Output (t)
3	
4	

3. What is the output value if the input value is 3? _____

4. What is the output value if the input value is 4? _____

Rule: $r = q \div 3$

Input (q)	Output (r)
27	
	11

5. What is the output value if the input value is 27? _____

6. What is the input value if the output value is 11? _____

Hands On: Multiply 2-Digit Numbers by 1-Digit Numbers

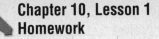

CA Standard
KEY NS 3.0

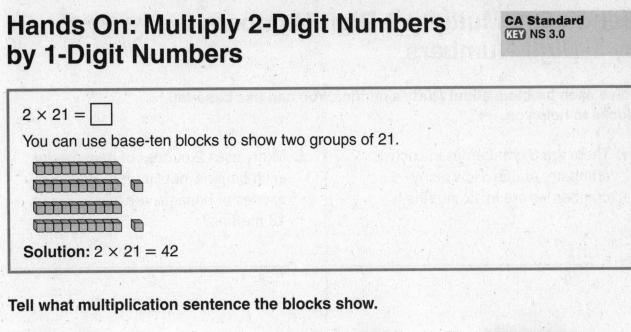

$2 \times 21 = \square$

You can use base-ten blocks to show two groups of 21.

Solution: $2 \times 21 = 42$

Tell what multiplication sentence the blocks show.

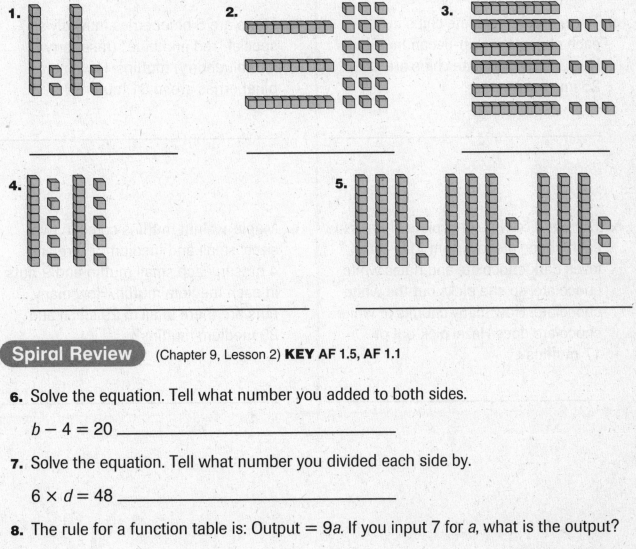

1. _____

2. _____

3. _____

4. _____

5. _____

Spiral Review (Chapter 9, Lesson 2) **KEY** AF 1.5, AF 1.1

6. Solve the equation. Tell what number you added to both sides.

   $b - 4 = 20$ _____

7. Solve the equation. Tell what number you divided each side by.

   $6 \times d = 48$ _____

8. The rule for a function table is: Output = 9*a*. If you input 7 for *a*, what is the output?

Hands On: Multiply 2-Digit Numbers by 1-Digit Numbers

Solve each problem about Muffy's muffins. You can use base-ten blocks to help you.

1. There are 3 cranberries in each cranberry muffin. How many cranberries are in 12 muffins?

_____

2. Muffy uses 2 ounces of bananas for each banana-nuts muffin. How many ounces of bananas are in 18 muffins?

_____

3. There are 6 chocolate chips in each chocolate chip-pecan muffin. How many chocolate chips are in 25 muffins?

_____

4. There are 5 blueberries in Muffy's special "red and blue" (raspberry and blueberry) muffins. How many blueberries are in 31 muffins?

_____

5. There are 5 white chocolate chunks in each chocolate lover's muffin. Hazel loves dark chocolate and hates white chocolate, so she picks out the white chocolate. How many chunks of white chocolate does Hazel pick out of 17 muffins?

_____

6. Maple-walnut muffins come in two sizes: small and medium. There are 4 nuts in each small muffin and 9 nuts in each medium muffin. How many nuts are there in all in 29 small and 29 medium muffins?

_____

Estimate Products

CA Standards
KEY NS 1.4, MR 2.5

Estimate 47×3.

47 rounds to 50.

$$47 \longrightarrow 50$$
$$\underline{\times 3} \longrightarrow \underline{\times 3}$$
$$150$$

Solution: 47×3 is about 150.

Round the larger number to the greatest place. Then estimate the product.

1. 39 $\times$ 9	**2.** 68 $\times$ 9	**3.** 62 $\times$ 4	**4.** 325 $\times$ 5

5. 79 $\times$ 8	**6.** 167 $\times$ 8	**7.** 725 $\times$ 8	**8.** 3,088 $\times$ 7

9. 4,722 $\times$ 6	**10.** 4×58	**11.** 7×62	**12.** 3×495

13. 6×678 **14.** $4 \times 4,298$

Spiral Review   (Chapter 6, Lesson 3) **KEY NS 3.0, AF 1.0**

Use multiplication properties and division rules to solve.

15. $1 \times 98 =$ _____

16. $98 \div 1 =$ _____

17. Alice has 5×6 ribbons. Change the order of the factors to show another way to tell how many ribbons Alice has.

_____

Estimate Products

CA Standards
KEY NS 1.4, MR 2.5

The California state flag has a grizzly bear on it. The table below gives the weight of the grizzly and other members of the bear family. Ursidae is the family that includes all bears, including those listed that are in various genus and species.

Bears	
Name	Weight (pounds)
Grizzly	704
Polar	1,595
Sloth	278
Brown	753
Kodiak	1,600
Giant Panda	220
Spectacled	343
Black	518

Use the table to solve each problem. Round the larger number to the greatest place. Then estimate the product.

1. About how many pounds do 5 sloth bears weigh?

   _____

2. About how many pounds do 8 black bears weigh?

   _____

3. About how many pounds do 4 brown bears and 3 grizzly bears weigh together?

   _____

4. About how many pounds do 6 giant pandas and 5 Kodiak bears weigh together?

   _____

5. About how many pounds more do 9 polar bears weigh than 9 spectacled bears?

   _____

6. Which weigh more: 8 grizzly bears or 7 brown bears?

   _____

   _____

Use with text pp. 216–218

Multiply Greater Numbers

CA Standards
KEY NS 3.0, MR 2.1

$1,825 \times 3 =$ _____

$$\begin{array}{r} {}^{2}\ {}^{1} \\ 1,825 \\ \times \quad 3 \\ \hline 5,475 \end{array}$$

- Multiply the ones.
- Multiply the tens.
- Multiply the hundreds.
- Multiply the thousands.

Solution: $1,825 \times 3 = 5,475$

Multiply. Check by estimation.

1. $\begin{array}{r} 258 \\ \times\ 2 \\ \hline \end{array}$

2. $\begin{array}{r} 662 \\ \times\ 5 \\ \hline \end{array}$

3. $\begin{array}{r} 452 \\ \times\ 3 \\ \hline \end{array}$

4. $\begin{array}{r} \$23.45 \\ \times\ 4 \\ \hline \end{array}$

5. $\begin{array}{r} 3,496 \\ \times\ 6 \\ \hline \end{array}$

6. $\begin{array}{r} 5,108 \\ \times\ 3 \\ \hline \end{array}$

7. $\begin{array}{r} 1,042 \\ \times\ 2 \\ \hline \end{array}$

8. $\begin{array}{r} 3,175 \\ \times\ 5 \\ \hline \end{array}$

9. $1,288 \times 2$

10. $\$32.17 \times 4$

11. $4,234 \times 5$

12. $\$64.25 \times 4$

_____   _____   _____   _____

Spiral Review   (Chapter 8, Lessons 3–4) **KEY** AF 2.0, **KEY** AF 2.1, **KEY** AF 2.2

13. Solve the equation. Tell what number you subtracted from both sides.

   $5 + f = 38$ _____

14. Solve the equation. Tell what number you multiplied both sides by.

   $k \div 6 = 6$ _____

15. Lee found 7 new rocks for his collection. Now he has a total of 23 rocks.
    Write an equation to show how many rocks Lee started with.

_____

Multiply Greater Numbers

CA Standards
KEY NS 3.0, MR 2.1

Use the price list to solve each problem.

Ike & Izzy's Ice Cream Cones	
Scoops	Price
1	$1.27
5	$6.22
10	$12.36
15	$18.05
20	$24.73

Sprinkles: 34¢ extra for each scoop

1. 8 people bought 1-scoop cones. How much did they pay in all?

_____

2. 6 people bought 10-scoop cones. How much did they pay in all?

_____

3. 5 people bought 1-scoop cones and 2 people bought 20-scoop cones. How much did they pay in all?

_____

4. 3 people bought 5-scoop cones and 4 people bought 15-scoop cones. How much did they pay in all?

_____

5. 9 people bought 10-scoop cones. They all ordered sprinkles. How much did they pay in all?

_____

6. 4 people bought 15-scoop cones. 2 of them ordered sprinkles. 3 people bought 20-scoop cones. 1 of them ordered sprinkles. How much did they pay in all?

_____

Multiply with Zeros

CA Standards
KEY NS 3.0, MR 2.1

$3 \times 207 =$ _____

$\overset{2}{}$
$\begin{array}{r} 207 \\ \times\ \ 3 \\ \hline 621 \end{array}$

• Multiply the ones.
• Multiply the tens. Add the regrouped 2.
• Multiply the hundreds.

Solution: $3 \times 207 = 621$

Multiply. Check by estimation.

1. $\begin{array}{r} 650 \\ \times\ \ 4 \\ \hline \end{array}$

2. $\begin{array}{r} 501 \\ \times\ \ 8 \\ \hline \end{array}$

3. $\begin{array}{r} 2,807 \\ \times\ \ \ \ 2 \\ \hline \end{array}$

4. $\begin{array}{r} 3,005 \\ \times\ \ \ \ 5 \\ \hline \end{array}$

5. $\begin{array}{r} 8,130 \\ \times\ \ \ \ 2 \\ \hline \end{array}$

6. $\begin{array}{r} 4,040 \\ \times\ \ \ \ 4 \\ \hline \end{array}$

7. $\begin{array}{r} 2,700 \\ \times\ \ \ \ 6 \\ \hline \end{array}$

8. $\begin{array}{r} 1,095 \\ \times\ \ \ \ 9 \\ \hline \end{array}$

9. 208×3

10. 500×4

11. $2,106 \times 5$

12. $4,078 \times 3$

_____ _____ _____ _____

Spiral Review (Chapter 9, Lesson 2) **KEY** AF 1.5, AF 1.1

Use the function table to answer the questions.

13. What input (value) gives an output of 24?

_____

14. When you input 13, what is the output?

_____

Rule: Output = $a \times 3$	
Input (*a*)	Output
5	15
?	24
13	?

15. In a function table, the input (*a*) is 10 and the
output is 30. What are two possible rules?

Output = _____

Output = _____

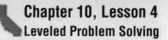
Multiply with Zeros

CA Standards
KEY NS 3.0, MR 2.1

Multiply to solve each problem.

1. A store has 540 T-shirts in each of 3 colors. How many T-shirts are there in all?

_____

2. There are 805 pairs of sneakers in each of 6 sizes. How many pairs of sneakers are there in all?

_____

3. There are 1,060 caps in each of 4 colors. How many caps are there in all?

_____

4. There are 8,009 flags for each of 5 school teams. How many flags are there in all?

_____

5. There are 2,099 girls' bathing suits in each of 7 colors and 1,806 boys' bathing suits in each of 5 colors. How many bathing suits are there in all?

_____

6. There are 2,300 size-10 sweatshirts in each of 3 colors. And there are 1,600 size-12 sweatshirts in each of 2 colors. How many sweatshirts are there in all?

_____

Hands On: Multiply by Multiples of 10

Use basic facts and patterns to find the products.

$6 \times 4 = 24$ $60 \times 4 = 240$ $60 \times 40 = 2,400$ $600 \times 40 = 24,000$ $6,000 \times 40 = 240,000$

- Use the basic fact.
  $6 \times 4 = 24$
- Count the number of zeros in the factors.
- Write that number of zeros to the right of 24.

1. 5×5 _____

  50×5 _____

  500×5 _____

  $5,000 \times 5$ _____

2. 4×9 _____

  40×9 _____

  400×9 _____

  $4,000 \times 9$ _____

3. 2×8 _____

  20×8 _____

  200×8 _____

  $2,000 \times 8$ _____

4. 50×6 _____

5. 80×80 _____

6. 700×50 _____

7. $4,000 \times 40$ _____

Spiral Review (Chapter 2, Lesson 3) **KEY NS 1.3**

8. Round each number to the nearest hundred. Then estimate the difference.
  6,710
  −4,823

9. Round each number to the nearest thousand. Then estimate the difference.
  8,562
  −3,401

10. Beanbags R Us had 12,756 beans. They put 8,499 beans in beanbags. Round each number to the nearest thousand. Then estimate how many beans are left.

_____

Hands On: Multiply by Multiples of 10

CA Standards
KEY NS 3.0, KEY NS 3.3

Use basic facts and patterns to find the products.

1. At the Stockton Asparagus Festival, Elena bought 30 spears of asparagus. What is 700 times that number?

   _____

2. There were 70 balloons at the Great California Balloon Challenge in Bakersfield. What is 60 times that number?

   _____

3. At the Strawberry Festival in Arroyo Grande, 600 bushels of strawberries were sold. What is 400 times that number?

   _____

4. At the Lodi Grape Festival, Maggie sold 50 pints of grapes. What is 3,000 times that number?

   _____

5. At the Old Spanish Days Fiesta in Santa Barbara, there were 118 piñatas shaped like donkeys and 82 piñatas shaped like pigs. What is 900 times the total number of piñatas?

   _____

6. At the Clam Festival in Pismo Beach, there were small, medium, and large size clams. Henry ate 10 small clams, 8 medium clams, and 7 large clams. What is 4,000 times the total number of clams Henry ate?

   _____

Use with text pp. 234–235

Name _____ Date _____

Hands On: Multiply 2-Digit Numbers by 2-Digit Numbers

CA Standards
AF 1.0, KEY NS 3.3

Use models and the Distributive Property to find each product.

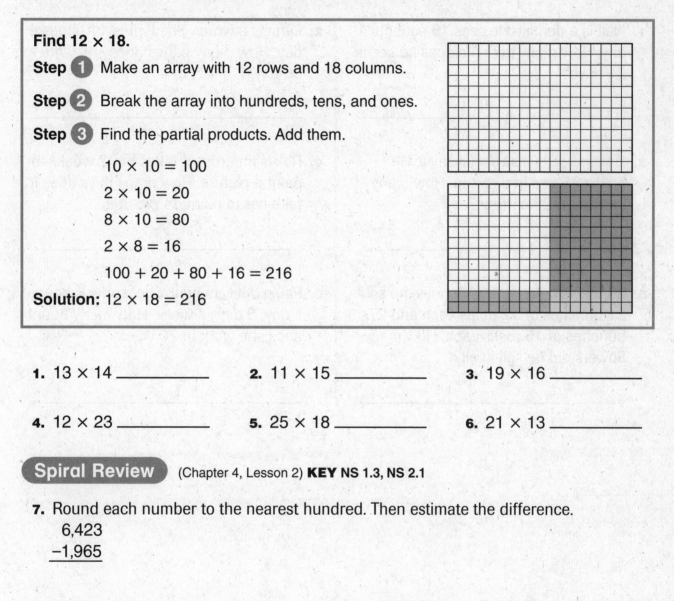

Find 12 × 18.

Step 1 Make an array with 12 rows and 18 columns.

Step 2 Break the array into hundreds, tens, and ones.

Step 3 Find the partial products. Add them.

$10 \times 10 = 100$

$2 \times 10 = 20$

$8 \times 10 = 80$

$2 \times 8 = 16$

$100 + 20 + 80 + 16 = 216$

Solution: $12 \times 18 = 216$

1. 13×14 _____   **2.** 11×15 _____   **3.** 19×16 _____

4. 12×23 _____   **5.** 25×18 _____   **6.** 21×13 _____

Spiral Review (Chapter 4, Lesson 2) **KEY** NS 1.3, NS 2.1

7. Round each number to the nearest hundred. Then estimate the difference.

6,423
−1,965

8. Round each number to the nearest thousand. Then estimate the difference.

21,295
−20,844

9. Ryan had 968 bushels of tomatoes. He sold 545 bushels. Round each number to the nearest hundred. Then estimate how many bushels Ryan has left.

_____

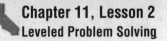
Hands On: Multiply 2-Digit Numbers by 2-Digit Numbers

CA Standards
AF 1.0, (KEY) NS 3.3

Use models and the Distributive Property to solve the problems.

1. Neil is a dentist. He sees 16 patients a day. How many patients does he see in 21 days?

   _____

2. Lana is a writer. She writes 11 pages a day. How many pages does she write in 36 days?

   _____

3. Howard sells his special salsa. He packs 25 jars in a carton. How many jars are in 28 cartons?

   _____

4. Roz is an artist. It takes her 2 weeks to paint a picture. How many days does it take her to paint 44 pictures?

   _____

5. Miguel is a florist. On Monday, he sold 21 bunches of 12 tulips each and 27 bunches of 15 roses each. How many flowers did he sell in all?

   _____

6. Paula delivers mail. She works 8 hours a day, 5 days a week. How many hours does she work in 26 weeks?

   _____

Multiply 2-Digit Numbers by 2-Digit Numbers

CA Standards
KEY NS 3.2, KEY NS 3.3

Find 15 × 13.

Multiply by the ones.	Multiply by the tens.	Add the products.
$\begin{array}{r} 1 \\ 15 \\ \times\ 13 \\ \hline 45 \end{array}$	$\begin{array}{r} 1 \\ 15 \\ \times\ 13 \\ \hline 45 \\ 150 \\ \hline \end{array}$	$\begin{array}{r} 1 \\ 15 \\ \times\ 13 \\ \hline 45 \\ +\ 150 \\ \hline 195 \end{array}$

Solution: 15 × 13 = 195

Multiply.

1. $\begin{array}{r} 76 \\ \times\ 51 \\ \hline \end{array}$

2. $\begin{array}{r} 23 \\ \times\ 80 \\ \hline \end{array}$

3. $\begin{array}{r} 31 \\ \times\ 31 \\ \hline \end{array}$

4. $\begin{array}{r} 24 \\ \times\ 32 \\ \hline \end{array}$

5. $\begin{array}{r} 45 \\ \times\ 37 \\ \hline \end{array}$

6. $\begin{array}{r} 62 \\ \times\ 51 \\ \hline \end{array}$

7. $\begin{array}{r} 15 \\ \times\ 70 \\ \hline \end{array}$

8. $\begin{array}{r} 55 \\ \times\ 90 \\ \hline \end{array}$

9. $\begin{array}{r} 18 \\ \times\ 18 \\ \hline \end{array}$

Spiral Review (Chapter 9, Lesson 3) **KEY AF 1.5, AF 1.1**

10. Complete the function table.

Rule: $y = 2x - 7$

Input (x)	Output (y)
5	3
13	19
50	

11. Write the rule.

Rule: _____

Input (a)	Output (b)
6	18
21	63
49	147

12. The rule of a function table is $b = a \div 6$. If the input (a) is 54, what is the output (b)?

Multiply 2-Digit Numbers by 2-Digit Numbers

CA Standards
KEY NS 3.2, **KEY** NS 3.3

A small crafts store in Anaheim called **I'm Crazy About Colors!** sells boxes of markers in five sizes.

Box Sizes	Number of Markers per Box
Small	11
Medium	36
Large	54
Extra-large	78
Super-duper	99

Use the table to solve each problem.

1. On Monday, the store sold 18 medium boxes of markers. How many markers were sold in all?

   _____

2. On Tuesday, the store sold 73 small boxes of markers. How many markers were sold in all?

   _____

3. On Wednesday, the store sold 12 large boxes and 11 medium boxes of markers. How many markers were sold in all?

   _____

4. On Thursday, the store sold 20 extra-large boxes and 38 super-duper boxes of markers. How many markers were sold in all?

   _____

5. How many more markers are in 75 small boxes than in 21 medium boxes?

   _____

6. How many more markers are in 99 large boxes than in 53 super-duper boxes?

   _____

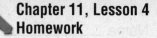
Multiply 3-Digit Numbers by 2-Digit Numbers

CA Standards
KEY NS 3.2, **KEY** NS 3.3

Find 115 × 13.		
Multiply by the ones.	Multiply by the tens.	Add the products.
$\begin{array}{r} 1 \\ 115 \\ \times\ 13 \\ \hline 345 \end{array}$	$\begin{array}{r} 1 \\ 115 \\ \times\ 13 \\ \hline 345 \\ 1150 \end{array}$	$\begin{array}{r} 1 \\ 115 \\ \times\ 13 \\ \hline 345 \\ +1150 \\ \hline 1{,}495 \end{array}$
		Solution: 115 × 13 = 1,495

Multiply.

1. 222
    × 26

2. 304
    × 28

3. 136
    × 34

4. 316
    × 14

5. 182
    × 21

6. 409
    × 24

7. 179 × 52

8. 235 × 36

9. 501 × 15

10. 326 × 57

_____ _____ _____ _____

Spiral Review (Chapter 10, Lesson 2) **KEY** NS 1.4, MR 2.5

Round the larger number to the greatest place. Then estimate the product.

11. 726
    × 4

12. 865
    × 6

13. Last year, 528 people took the test for the police academy. This year, 3 times as many people took the test. Estimate the number of people who took the test this year.

_____

Multiply 3-Digit Numbers by 2-Digit Numbers

Multiply.

1. It takes Mercury 88 days to orbit the Sun. How many days does it take for Mercury to orbit the sun 100 times?

   _____

2. Venus orbits the Sun in 225 days. How many days does it take Venus to orbit the Sun 11 times?

   _____

3. Saturn orbits the Sun in 29 years. How many years does it take Saturn to orbit the sun 426 times?

   _____

4. It takes Jupiter 12 years to orbit the Sun. How many *days* does it take Jupiter to orbit the Sun? Add 3 days for leap years.

   _____

5. Pluto is a dwarf planet. Its orbit is slower than any of the planets in our solar system. It takes 248 years to orbit the Sun. How many years does Pluto take to orbit the Sun 99 times?

   _____

6. Mars is 128 million miles from the Sun. It takes Mars 687 days to orbit the Sun. How many days does it take Mars to orbit the Sun 88 times?

   _____

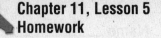
Problem Solving: Guess and Check

CA Standards
MR 1.0, **KEY** NS 3.3

> Yvette is thinking of two numbers. The product of the two numbers is 3,840.
> Their difference is 224. What are the two numbers Yvette is thinking of?
>
> Think about what you know. Use the problem-solving strategy Guess and Check to find
> the two numbers.
>
> Think of numbers that have a product of 40. Find the difference of the numbers.
>
> | First Number | Second Number | Product | Difference | |
> |---|---|---|---|---|
> | 480 | 8 | 3,840 | 472 | X |
> | 320 | 12 | 3,840 | 308 | X |
> | 240 | 16 | 3,840 | 224 | ✓ |
>
> The numbers Yvette is thinking of are 240 and 16.

Use Guess and Check to solve each problem.

1. Jeremy wrote down two numbers.
The product of the two numbers is 12.
Their difference is 4. What are the two
numbers Jeremy wrote down?

_____

2. Mandy is thinking of two numbers.
The product of the two numbers is 36.
Their difference is 9. What are the two
numbers Mandy is thinking of?

_____

Spiral Review (Chapter 10, Lesson 2) **KEY** NS 1.4, MR 2.5

**Round the larger number to the greatest place. Then estimate
the product.**

3. 525 × 8 = _____

4. 721 × 9 = _____

5. Yvette, Jeremy, and Mandy were asked to find the product of 327 × 6. Yvette said
the product was 1,562. Jeremy said the product was 1,962. Mandy said the product
was 3,162. Whose product is correct? Use estimation to decide. Explain your
reasoning.

_____

_____

_____

_____

Homework

99

Use with text pp. 246–247

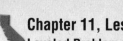
Problem Solving: Guess and Check

CA Standards
MR 1.0, **KEY** NS 3.3

Use Guess and Check to solve the problems.

1. Trinity is thinking of two numbers. The product of the two numbers is 36. The sum of the two numbers is 15. What are the two numbers?

_____

2. The product of two numbers is 48. The difference between the numbers is 8. What are the numbers?

_____

3. The movie theater charges $4.00 for each child ticket and $7.00 for each adult ticket. The art club purchased a total of 20 tickets and spent $101.00. How many of each type of ticket did the club buy?

_____

_____

4. A bicycle shop has bicycles with 2 wheels and tricycles with 3 wheels. They have 15 different cycles for sale. The 15 cycles have 34 wheels. How many bicycles and tricycles does the shop have for sale?

_____

_____

5. A museum cashier collected $78 in fees. He collected only $5 and $1 bills. He collected 18 bills in all. How many of each kind of bill did the cashier collect?

_____

_____

6. David's novel has 12 chapters. Some of the chapters have 25 pages and some of the chapters have 37 pages. How many of each size chapter does the novel have if it is 360 pages long?

_____

_____

Name _____ Date _____

Hands On: Model Division

CA Standard
KEY NS 3.0

Use base-ten blocks to complete the table.

Number	Number of Equal Groups	Number in Each Group
27	2	13
		Number Left
		1
		Number Sentence
		$27 \div 2 = 13$ R1

	Number	Number of Equal Groups	Number in Each Group	Number Left	Number Sentence
1.	35	6			
2.	18	5			
3.	81		9		
4.	59	7			

Spiral Review (Chapter 7, Lessons 2 and 4) **KEY AF 1.2, KEY 1.3**

Write an expression for each situation.

5. 13 fewer than 5 times 4

6. 62 more than 20 divided by 5

_____

_____

Write and evaluate an expression to answer the question.

7. Bobby read 20 pages of a book one week. He read 3 times as many pages the following week. How many pages did he read in the 2 weeks?

_____

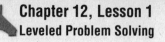
Hands On: Model Division

The students were organizing items for a school garage sale to raise money for a new playground. Solve each problem.

1. Benita had 30 CDs that people had donated to the garage sale. She divided them into 3 equal groups. How many CDs were in each group?

   _____

2. Earl and Marcia put 80 old record albums into 4 boxes with an equal number in each box. How many records were in each box?

   _____

3. There were 42 hardcover books to sell. Angel displayed them in 5 equal stacks on a table. How many stacks were there and how many books were left over?

   _____

4. There were 106 paperbacks books on sale. Benita came up with a good way to sell them. She placed 10 books each in bags and sold each bag for $2. How many bags of books did she make and how many books were left over?

   _____

5. Marcia collected a number of used DVDs for the sale. There were 12 action movies, 7 comedies, and 8 animated films. She decided to put them on sale at 3 for $5. How many groups of 3 DVDs went on sale? How much money did they bring in?

   _____

6. When the sale ended, there were 10 hardcover books, 26 paperback books and 6 CDs that didn't sell. The students decided to donate them to 3 area children hospitals. If the items were divided equally, how many books and CDs will each hospital receive?

   _____

Divide Larger Numbers with Remainders

$49 \div 4$

Step 1
$$4\overline{)49} \quad \begin{array}{l} 1 \\ \hline \end{array}$$
$$-4$$
$$\overline{0}$$

Multiply 1 ten × 4.
Subtract 4 − 4.
Compare 0 < 4.

Step 2
$$4\overline{)49} \quad \begin{array}{l} 12 \text{ R1} \\ \hline \end{array}$$
$$-4\downarrow$$
$$\overline{09}$$
$$-8$$
$$\overline{1}$$

Bring down 9 ones.
Multiply 2 ones × 4.
Subtract 9 − 8.
Compare 1 < 4.

Solution: $49 \div 4 = 12$ R1

Divide. Use multiplication to check.

1. $3\overline{)64}$

2. $4\overline{)88}$

3. $3\overline{)37}$

4. $4\overline{)86}$

5. $58 \div 5$

6. $35 \div 3$

7. $49 \div 4$

8. $77 \div 7$

_____ _____ _____ _____

Spiral Review (Chapter 7, Lesson 3) **AF 1.0**

Copy and complete using >, <, or =.

9. $2 + 8 \times 4 \bigcirc 6 + (80 \div 4)$

_____

10. $2 \times 7 - 3 \bigcirc 33 \div 3$

_____

11. Marc swam 18 laps in the pool. Nona swam half as many laps as Marc. Les swam 7 fewer laps than Marc. Write a number sentence that compares how many laps Nona swam, to how many laps Les swam.

_____

Divide Larger Numbers with Remainders

CA Standards
KEY NS 3.2, KEY NS 3.0

Jane and her relatives had a family reunion picnic. Everyone brought something to eat. Use the facts to solve each problem.

1. One relative brought 5 watermelons to the picnic. When cut up, they made 60 slices of watermelon. If the melons were the same size, how many slices came from each watermelon?

   _____

2. Jane and her mother made turkey sandwiches for the picnic. If they had 140 slices of bread, how many sandwiches could they make?

   _____

3. There were 68 family members at the picnic. Most of them came in minibuses. If 8 people could fit in each minibus, how many minibuses did they need? How many people had to drive separately?

   _____

   _____

4. There were 216 cups of lemonade served at the picnic. If there were 9 jugs of lemonade, how many cups did each jug hold?

   _____

5. Jane's uncle stopped on the way to the picnic and bought 4 bags of fruit. He had $47 and after the purchase he had $3 left. How much did each bag of fruit cost him?

   _____

6. During the picnic, the 68 family members were joined by 14 more people. They sat and ate at 6 long tables. What equal number of people could fit at each table and how many people had to stand and eat?

   _____

Regroup in Division

Divide. Check your answers using multiplication and addition.

```
   13 R2
3)41
  -3↓
   11      Regroup the one ten
  - 9      left as 10 ones.
    2
```

Check:

$13 \times 3 = 39$

$39 + 2 = 41$

Solution: $41 \div 3 = 13$ R2

1. $6)\overline{66}$

2. $5)\overline{71}$

3. $53 \div 4$

_____

4. $38 \div 2$

_____

5. $79 \div 6$

_____

6. $95 \div 3$

_____

7. $44 \div 4$

_____

8. $74 \div 5$

_____

9. $61 \div 3$

_____

10. $33 \div 2$

_____

11. $84 \div 3$

_____

12. $58 \div 4$

_____

Spiral Review (Chapter 10, Lesson 3) **KEY** NS 3.0, MR 2.1

Multiply. Check by estimation.

13. 287×5

_____

14. $4,901 \times 3$

_____

15. Ben has 3 stamp albums. Each album has spaces for 1,022 stamps.
How many stamps could Ben mount in his 3 albums?

_____

Regroup in Division

Solve each problem.

1. There were 38 computers in the school computer lab. Half of them are not connected to the Internet. How many computers are connected to the Internet?

   _____

2. Darron's school has 54 computers for students to use. That is twice as many as are available at June's school. How many computers are there at June's school?

   _____

3. The school board ordered 40 new printers to be distributed in equal numbers to 3 schools. How many printers will each school receive? How many will be left over?

   _____

4. Along with the printers, the school board has ordered 74 reams of computer paper to be divided among the 3 schools. How many reams will each school receive and how many will be left over?

   _____

5. Each student in the fourth grade is given a pen at the start of the school year. There are 72 pens with black ink and 87 with blue ink. If the pens are divided equally among 5 fourth-grade classes, how many pens will each class receive? How many will be left over?

   _____

6. Each teacher can order 3 boxes of pencils for the school year. If three boxes together hold 72 pencils how many are in each box? If each class has 22 students, how many pencils can each student expect to receive for the year? How many will be left over?

   _____

Divide Multiples of 10

CA Standards
KEY NS 3.2, MR 1.1

Divide. Use multiplication to check.

$42 \div 6 = 7$
$420 \div 6 = 70$
↑ 1 zero   ↑ 1 zero
$4,200 \div 6 = 700$
↑ 2 zeros   ↑ 2 zeros

1. $9 \div 3 =$ _____
$90 \div 3 =$ _____
$900 \div 3 =$ _____

2. $4 \div 2 =$ _____
$40 \div 2 =$ _____
$400 \div 2 =$ _____

3. $6 \div 1 =$ _____
$60 \div 1 =$ _____
$600 \div 1 =$ _____
$6,000 \div 1 =$ _____

4. $12 \div 6 =$ _____
$120 \div 6 =$ _____
$1,200 \div 6 =$ _____
$12,000 \div 6 =$ _____

5. $21 \div 7 =$ _____
$210 \div 7 =$ _____
$2,100 \div 7 =$ _____
$21,000 \div 7 =$ _____

6. $3,600 \div 6 =$ _____

7. $420 \div 7 =$ _____

8. $350 \div 5 =$ _____

Solve each equation.

9. $2,500 \div 5 = x$

10. $180 \div y = 20$

11. $1,600 \div n = 800$

Spiral Review (Chapter 11, Lessons 2 and 3) **KEY NS 3.3**

Multiply.

12. 62×24

13. 83×17

14. A farmer sold 23 jugs of apple cider. If each jug held 128 ounces of cider, how many ounces of cider did he sell in all?

Divide Multiples of 10

CA Standards
KEY NS 3.2, MR 1.1

Solve each problem.

1. Ada collected 50 shells on the beach. She divided them equally into 10 display boxes. How many shells were in each box?

   _____

2. Sam collected 200 shells. He had 10 times as many shells as Mara does. How many shells did Mara find?

   _____

3. Ted collected 80 bits of colored glass at the beach. Juan collected 40 bits of glass. They combined their glass collections and divided them into 10 piles. How many pieces of glass were in each pile?

   _____

4. Lee-Anne looked for lost coins under the boardwalk at the beach. She found $2.40 in change. Hank also looked and found $1.80. Together they find 10 times as much money as Karl did. How much money did Karl find?

   _____

5. Terry guessed there were at least 60,000 grains of sand in a handful of sand. That was 100 times the number of grains he was able to actually count before giving up in desperation. How many grains of sand did Terry count?

   _____

6. There were 600 people at the beach on Saturday and another 900 who came on Sunday. The total number of people who came on the weekend was 5 times as many that came the remaining five days of that week. How many people came to the beach on the weekdays?

   _____

Problem Solving: Interpret Remainders

CA Standards
KEY NS 3.4, MR 1.0

Solve.

> A basket holds 4 dinner rolls. How many baskets are needed to hold
> 47 dinner rolls?
>
> **Divide.**
>
> ```
>   11 R3
> 4)47
>   −4
>   ──
>   07
>   − 4
>   ──
>    3
> ```
> There are enough rolls for 11 baskets. 3 rolls are left over.
>
> **Solution:** Another basket is needed to hold the 3 extra rolls, so 12 baskets are needed.

Solve each problem. Explain why your answer makes sense.

1. A florist received 59 roses. He wants to place the roses in buckets of water. Each bucket holds 5 roses. How many buckets will have 5 roses?

   _____

2. Ms. Dale bought 35 roses to give to her friends. She divided the roses equally among three friends and kept the leftover roses for herself. How many roses did Ms. Dale keep?

   _____

Spiral Review (Chapter 11, Lesson 2) **AF 1.0, KEY NS 3.3**

Use the Distributive Property to find the value of y.

3. $7y \times 4 = 21 \times 4$

4. $(5 + y) \times 12 = 8 \times 12$

   _____   _____

5. Mr. Webster bought a postcard collection. The collection included 12 books with 144 postcards in each book. How many postcards were in the collection?

   _____

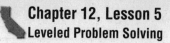
Problem Solving: Interpret Remainders

CA Standards
KEY NS 3.4, MR 1.0

Peter has 58 photos to put in an album. He plans to put 5 photos on each page. Help Peter figure out how many pages he will need.

1. Write a mathematical sentence that will tell how many pages he needs for all 58 photos. Use *p* for the answer.

_____

2. What is the remainder when you solve the mathematical sentence?

_____

3. How should you use this remainder to find out how many pages he will need?

_____

_____

_____

4. How many pages does Peter need?

_____

5. How many of the pages are full? How do you know?

_____

_____

_____

6. If Peter changes his plan and puts only 4 photos on each page, how many pages will be full and how many photos will be left over?

_____

_____

_____

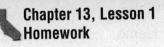
Hands On:
Model Division: 3-Digit Dividends

CA Standards
KEY NS 3.4, MR 2.3

How can you use base-ten blocks to divide 364 by 3?

Step **1** Divide the hundreds blocks into 3 equal groups.

Step **2** Divide the tens blocks into 3 equal groups.

Step **3** Divide the ones blocks into 3 equal groups.

Note there is 1 block left over, this is the remainder.

Solution: Each group has 1 hundred block, 2 tens blocks and 1 ones block, so 364 divided by 3 is $100 + 20 + 1 = 121$. Since there is 1 block leftover, the quotient is 121 R1.

Use base-ten blocks to find the following quotients.

1. $324 \div 4$ _____

2. $435 \div 3$ _____

3. $834 \div 2$ _____

4. $948 \div 5$ _____

5. $653 \div 7$ _____

6. $932 \div 2$ _____

Spiral Review (Chapter 11, Lesson 1) **KEY** NS 3.0, **KEY** NS 3.3

Multiply.

7. 400×4 _____

8. 60×70 _____

9. The auditorium at Roe Auditorium has 40 rows. If there are 30 seats in each row, how many seats are there in the auditorium?

_____

Hands On: Model Division: 3-Digit Dividends

CA Standards
KEY NS 3.4, MR 2.3

Solve.

1. Candace has 100 pieces of candy that she wants to give to her 5 friends. If each friend receives the same number of pieces, how many pieces of candy does each friend receive?

2. Galinda wants to read 240 pages of her favorite book by the end of the week. If there are 6 days left in the week, how many pages must she read per day?

3. Felix has 927 postage stamps. If 9 stamps are required to send each package, how many packages can Felix send?

4. Miranda wrote 184 words in 4 paragraphs. If each paragraph has the same number of words, how many words are in each paragraph?

5. Gabi has $218 to spend on 4 holiday gifts. If she were to divide the money equally on each gift, how much would each gift cost? How much money would she have left over?

6. Timani is dividing equally 822 marbles into 7 bags. Teo is dividing equally 485 marbles into 4 bags. Who will have more marbles leftover? How do you know?

3-Digit Quotients

CA Standards
KEY NS 3.4, KEY NS 3.0

Divide 3)547.	Remember the steps.	Solution:
	• Divide • Multiply • Subtract • Compare • Bring down	182 R1 3)547 −3↓ 24↓ −24 07 −6 1

Divide. Check your answers.

1. 3)428

2. 3)515

3. 5)842

4. 6)815

5. 3)705

6. 8)942

7. 8)987

8. 7)945

Spiral Review (Chapter 6, Lesson 2) **KEY** NS 3.0

Use the associated number sentence to fill in the box.

9. $\boxed{} \times 5 = 45$ $45 \div 5 = 9$

10. $12 \times \boxed{} = 60$ $60 \div 12 = 5$

11. Lauriann has 50 pieces of chocolate. If there are 10 pieces of chocolate in each box, how many boxes of chocolate does she have?

_____

3-Digit Quotients

CA Standards
KEY NS 3.0, KEY NS 3.4

Solve.

1. Mara's entire dessert contains 425 calories. If Mara eats 5 items for dessert, each containing the same number of calories, how many calories are in each item?

   _____

   _____

2. Galen used 120 ounces of toothpaste in 8 months. How many ounces of toothpaste did he use in each month?

   _____

   _____

3. Farhad used 128 thumbtacks to hang posters. If he used 4 thumbtacks to hang each poster, how many posters did he hang?

   _____

4. Sonja has $2.13 to spend on candy. If she buys candies for 5 cents each how many candies can she buy? How much money will she have leftover?

   _____

   _____

   _____

5. Arriana recorded the number of runs scored in each baseball game to be 10, 12, 16, 20, and 22. What is the average of the number of runs scored in a baseball game?

   _____

   _____

6. Anie's quiz scores were 82, 86, 90, and 94. What is the average of her scores?

   _____

Place the First Digit of the Quotient

CA Standards
KEY NS 3.2, **KEY** NS 3.4

Divide. Check your answers.

Divide $5\overline{)483}$.	Solution:
	$\begin{array}{r} 96 \text{ R3} \\ 5\overline{)483} \\ -45 \\ \hline 33 \\ -30 \\ \hline 3 \end{array}$ **Remember the steps:** • Estimate to place the first digit. • Divide the tens. • Bring down the ones. • Divide the ones.

1. $2\overline{)158}$

2. $3\overline{)164}$

3. $4\overline{)185}$ **4.** $6\overline{)560}$ **5.** $2\overline{)143}$ **6.** $6\overline{)416}$

Spiral Review   (Chapter 9, Lesson 3) **KEY AF 1.5, AF 1.1**

Copy and complete.

7. Rule: $y = 4x + 1$

Input (x)	Output (y)
2	☐
4	☐

8. Rule: $n = m + 5$

Input (m)	Output (n)
10	☐
15	☐

9. Terrance describes the amount of money made based on the number of hours worked by the function rule $y = 10h$. Given this function, how much money does Terrance earn for each hour worked? Explain.

_____

_____

Place the First Digit of the Quotient

Solve.

1. Max has 602 pennies. If he divides his pennies in half and gives half of them to his brother, how many pennies do Max and his brother each have?

   _____

2. Five friends spent $510 on a vacation. If the cost of the vacation was split evenly, how much did each friend spend on the vacation?

   _____

   _____

3. Last year, Kristen spent 728 minutes watching movies. If she watched 7 movies of the same length, how long was each movie?

   _____

4. Mei went to the store to buy 120 rolls of paper towels If she bought 3 containers of paper towels, how many rolls of paper towels are in each container?

   _____

   _____

5. Britney, Jamie-Lynn, Kevin, and Sean split the cost of a pizza evenly. If the pizza cost $9.40, how much did each person pay?

   _____

   _____

6. Ben and Joe are each traveling 960 miles. Ben divides the trip into 6 equal parts, and Joe divides the trip into 8 equal parts. How many more miles is each part of Ben's trip than each part of Joe's trip?

   _____

Zeros in the Quotient

Divide. Check your answers.

1. $2\overline{)612}$

Divide. $3\overline{)626}$

```
    208 R2
3)626
  -6
   02
   -0
   026
  -24
    2
```

Remember the steps:
- Decide where to place the first digit.
- Bring down the tens. Divide the tens.
- Bring down the ones. Divide the ones.

Solution: 208 R2

2. $6\overline{)655}$

3. $4\overline{)836}$ 4. $7\overline{)762}$ 5. $2\overline{)813}$ 6. $6\overline{)485}$

7. $3\overline{)921}$ 8. $2\overline{)417}$ 9. $5\overline{)353}$ 10. $4\overline{)419}$

11. $512 \div 5$ 12. $735 \div 7$ 13. $101 \div 2$ 14. $622 \div 3$

_____   _____   _____   _____

Spiral Review   (Chapter 12, Lessons 2 and 3) **KEY** NS 3.0, **KEY** NS 3.2

Divide. Check your answers.

15. $5\overline{)34}$ 16. $9\overline{)56}$

17. Gianna is placing 23 books onto 4 shelves. If each shelf holds the same number of books, how many books are leftover?

_____

Name _____ Date _____

Zeros in the Quotient

Solve.

1. Alexa ran 4 laps around the school track, running a total of 800 meters. How many meters is each lap of the track?

_____

2. Vishal used 160 airtime minutes in one week. If these minutes were evenly distributed among 8 phone calls, how many minutes did each call last?

_____

3. Herman has 104 socks he is folding into pairs. How many pairs of socks will be make?

_____

4. Tony baked 218 cookies. He placed them into bags of 2 cookies each. How many bags did he make?

_____

5. Lexi is putting photos in her album. She puts 4 photos on each page. She has 263 summer photos and 165 winter photos. How many pages will she use for her pictures?

_____

6. Flowers cost $10.00 per half-dozen (6) plus $2.00 for each individual flower. If Billy wanted to buy 304 flowers, how much would it cost?

_____

Leveled Problem Solving
118
Use with text pp. 290–291

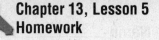

Problem Solving: Find an Average

The aquarium has numerous tanks in which fish and other sea life live and are displayed. One tank holds 110 gallons of water. Another tank holds 125 gallons. A third holds 150 gallons and a fourth 115 gallons. What is the average amount of water in the four tanks?

Step 1 Add all the amounts of water in the tanks.

110 ← addend 1
125 ← addend 2
150 ← addend 3
115 ← addend 4
500 ← sum

Step 2 Divide the total gallons of water by the number of tanks.

$500 \div 4 = 125$

Solution: The average amount of water in the tanks is 125 gallons.

Find the average to solve each problem.

1. The aquarium has five kinds of sharks in the shark room. The mako shark is 10 feet long. The white shark is 22 feet long. The length of the hammerhead shark is 13 feet and the thresher shark measures 18 feet. The nurse shark is 12 feet long. What is the average length of the sharks?

   _____

2. The big game-fish tank is one of the most popular attractions at the aquarium. The biggest fish in this tank are a blue marlin weighing 280 pounds, a sailfish weighing 120 pounds, a swordfish weighing 240 pounds, and a white marlin weighing 140 pounds. What is the average weight of these fish?

   _____

3. During school vacation week, 300 visitors came to the aquarium on Monday, 350 on Tuesday, 425 on Wednesday, and 557 on Thursday. What is the average attendance for these four days?

   _____

Problem Solving: Find an Average

CA Standards
KEY NS 3.4, MR 2.6

Solve. Explain why the average is or is not reasonable.

1. There are 4 fourth-grade classes. They have the following numbers of students: 24, 25, 20, 23. What is the average number of students in all 4 classes?

   _____

   _____

2. Jenny's rabbit weighs 8 lb. Her cat weighs 14 lb and her dog weighs 53 lb. What is the average weight of all 3 pets?

   _____

   _____

   _____

3. Earl does yard work for his neighbors every summer. This year he earned $425 in of June, $262 in July, and $327 in August. How much money did he earn on average for each month?

   _____

   _____

   _____

4. Mina ran 6 miles on Monday, 7 on Tuesday, 5 on Wednesday, and 3 in the morning and 4 in the afternoon on Thursday. She did not run on Friday. What was the average number of miles each day?

   _____

   _____

   _____

5. Sam read 40 pages of his book one week, 62 the next week, and 54 the third week. Dina read 51 pages of her book the first week, 38 the second, and 49 the third. Who read the greater number of average pages per week?

   _____

   _____

   _____

6. Three boys measured their heights. Alex is 62 inches tall. James is 68 inches tall. If the average height of the 3 boys is 64 inches, how tall is Bob?

   _____

   _____

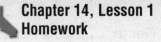
Hands On: Find Factors of a Number

CA Standards
NS 4.0, NS 4.1

Lexi has collected 6 buttons. She wishes to display the buttons in an array. What different arrays can she make? What are the factors of 6?

Step 1 Use 6 counters to make an array with 1 row and 6 columns. Record the array by labeling the number of rows and the number of columns.

Step 2 Use the number of rows and columns to write a multiplication expression that represents the array.

1×6

Step 3 Repeat step 1 using an array with 2 rows, an array with 3 rows, and an array with 6 rows.

1×6 2×3 3×2 6×1

Solution: Lexi can arrange her 6 buttons in four different arrays. The factors of 6 are 1, 2, 3, and 6.

Use counters to make arrays that help you answer the following questions.

1. What arrays can you make to show the factors of 3? What are the factors of 3?

_____

2. What arrays can you make to show the factors of 4? What are the factors of 4?

_____

Spiral Review   (Chapter 6, Lesson 4) **KEY NS 3.0**

Complete each multiplication expression by adding the correct factor.

3. $2 \times \bigcirc = 8$

4. $\bigcirc \times 3 = 6$

5. How many multiplication expressions can you write for the number 4?

_____

Name _____ Date _____

Hands On: Find Factors of a Number

CA Standards
NS 4.0, NS 4.1

Use counters to make arrays that help you answer the following questions.

1. What arrays can you make to show the factors of 2?

_____

2. What are the factors of 2?

_____

3. What arrays can you make to show the factors of 16?

_____

_____

4. What are the factors of 16?

_____

5. What arrays can you make to show the factors of 24?

_____

_____

6. What are the factors of 24?

_____

Name _____ Date _____

Divisibility Rules

CA Standards
NS 4.0, NS 4.1

Use divisibility rules to tell if 2, 3, 5, 9, and 10 are the factors of 38.

Step 1 To determine factors of 38, you may refer to a multiplication table. Since 38 is an even number, it is divisible by 2. So, 2 is a factor of 38.

Step 2 Since 38 does not end in 0 or 5, it does not have 5 or 10 as a factor.

Step 3 The sum of the digits 3 and 8 is 11, which is not divisible by 3 or by 9.

Solution: 2 is a factor of 38.

Use divisibility rules to tell if 2, 3, 5, 9, and 10 are factors of the given numbers.

1. 39

_____

2. 55

_____

3. 72

_____

4. 90

_____

Spiral Review   (Chapter 8, Lesson 4) **KEY AF 2.0, KEY AF 2.2**

Solve the equations.

5. $6x = 48$ _____   **6.** $y \div 7 = 11$ _____

7. The book shop has 63 rare books on display. If there are 9 rare books in each display case, how many display cases are being used for rare books?

_____

Divisibility Rules

Use divisibility rules to answer the following questions.

1. Which of the numbers 2, 3, 5, 9, and 10 are factors of 20?

   _____

2. Which of the numbers 2, 3, 5, 9, and 10 are factors of 32?

   _____

3. Which of the numbers 2, 3, 5, 9, and 10 are factors of 94?

   _____

4. Which of the numbers 2, 3, 5, 9, and 10 are factors of 108?

   _____

5. Which of the numbers 2, 3, 5, 9, and 10 are factors of 300?

   _____

6. Which of the numbers 2, 3, 5, 9, and 10 are factors of 2,340?

   _____

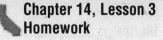
Prime and Composite Numbers

CA Standards
KEY NS 4.2, NS 4.1

List the factors for 2. Tell if the number is prime of composite.

Step ❶ To determine if a number is prime or composite, you can use counters to make arrays or you can use divisibility rules.

Step ❷ To determine if 2 is prime or composite, use counters.

With 2 counters, you can make only one array. 2 is a prime number because it has only two factors. These factors are 1 and 2.

Solution: $1 \times 2 = 2$

List the factors for each number. Use counters if you wish. Tell if the number is prime or composite.

	Number	Factors	Prime or Composite
1.	7		
2.	24		
3.	15		

Spiral Review (Chapter 12, Lesson 4) **KEY** NS 3.2, MR 1.1

Divide. Use multiplication to check.

4. $6 \div 3 =$ _____

$60 \div 3 =$ _____

5. $8 \div 2 =$ _____

$80 \div 2 =$ _____

6. Perry has 5 times as many seashells as she did three weeks ago. If she has 130 seashells now, how many seashells did Perry have three weeks ago?

_____

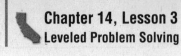
Prime and Composite Numbers

Use divisibility rules to answer the following questions.

1. Is the number 2 prime or composite, and what are its factors?

_____

2. Is the number 4 prime or composite, and what are its factors?

_____

3. Is the number 24 prime or composite, and what are its factors?

_____

_____

4. Is the number 23 prime or composite, and what are its factors?

_____

_____

5. Is the number 73 prime or composite, and what are its factors?

_____

6. Is the number 111 prime or composite, and what are its factors?

_____

_____

Factor Trees

CA Standards
KEY NS 4.2, NS 4.1

Make a factor tree for the number 18.

Step 1 Write any pair of factors for 18.

18
/ \
2 × 9

Step 2 Write a pair of factors for each factor until all the factors are prime numbers.

18
/ \
2 × 9
/ \
3 × 3

Solution: 2 × 3 × 3

Make a factor tree for each of the following numbers.

1. 15

_____

2. 28

_____

3. 45

_____

4. 70

_____

Spiral Review (Chapter 13, Lesson 3) **KEY NS 3.2, KEY NS 3.4**

Divide. Use multiplication to check.

5. 275 ÷ 5 = _____

6. 399 ÷ 7 = _____

7. Jamaal wants to sort 392 coins into 4 equal groups. How many coins will there be in each group?

_____

Homework

127

Use with text pp. 308–310

Name _____ Date _____

Factor Trees

CA Standards
KEY NS 4.2, NS 4.1

Make a factor tree for each number.

1. 14

_____

2. 20

_____

_____

_____

3. 44

_____

_____

4. 52

_____

_____

_____

5. 66

_____

_____

6. 81

_____

_____

_____

Hands On: Measure Length

Use a ruler to measure the length.

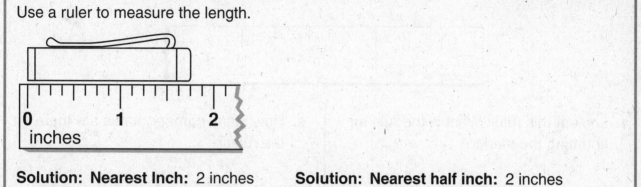

Solution: Nearest Inch: 2 inches   **Solution: Nearest half inch:** 2 inches

Measure to the nearest inch and half inch.

1.

_____

Estimate the length of each object to the nearest inch. Then measure to the nearest inch and half inch.

2.   GUM

_____

3.   ERASER

_____

Spiral Review   (Chapter 7, Lesson 2) **KEY AF 1.2, KEY AF 1.3**

Write an expression for each situation.

4. 32 fewer than 4 times 6 _____

5. 25 more than 72 divided by 8 _____

6. Mrs. Duffy's class is collecting bottle caps. Mrs. Duffy collected 25 bottle caps. One group of students collected 9 bags of bottle caps with 24 bottle caps in each bag. The second group collected twice as many bottle caps as Mrs. Duffy. How many bottle caps were collected? _____

Use with text pp. 326–327

Name _____ Date _____

Hands On: Measure Length

CA Standard
KEY NS 1.9

Solve each problem.

1. Look at this ruler. What is the rule for counting the marks?

_____

2. How many number marks are there on the ruler?

_____

3. What mark on a ruler is exactly halfway between 2 inches and 3 inches?

_____

4. What mark on a ruler is exactly halfway between 2 inches and 4 inches?

_____

5. Matt says this pencil is about 3 inches long. Do you agree? Explain your answer.

_____

_____

_____

_____

_____

6. Carla used a ruler to measure this marker. She says it is 4 inches long. What has she done wrong?

_____

_____

_____

_____

_____

Name _____ Date _____

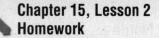
Perimeter and Customary Units of Length

CA Standards
KEY NS 3.2, MG 1.0

Find the perimeter of each polygon.

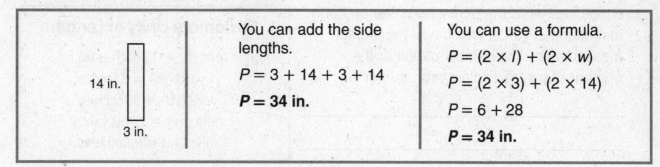

You can add the side lengths.

$P = 3 + 14 + 3 + 14$

P = 34 in.

You can use a formula.

$P = (2 \times l) + (2 \times w)$

$P = (2 \times 3) + (2 \times 14)$

$P = 6 + 28$

P = 34 in.

Write a formula to find each perimeter. Then solve.

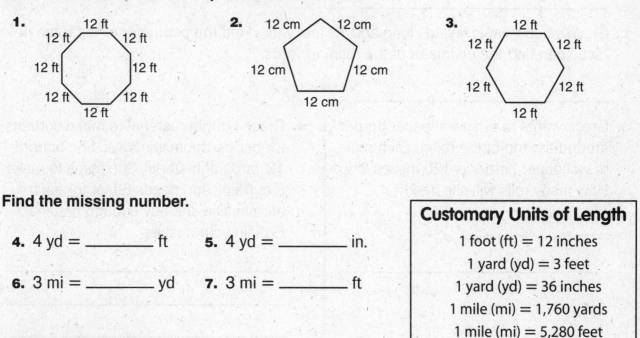

1.

12 ft
12 ft   12 ft
12 ft   12 ft
12 ft   12 ft
12 ft   12 ft
12 ft

2.

12 cm   12 cm
12 cm   12 cm
12 cm

3.

12 ft
12 ft   12 ft
12 ft   12 ft
12 ft

Find the missing number.

Customary Units of Length

4. 4 yd = _____ ft   **5.** 4 yd = _____ in.

6. 3 mi = _____ yd   **7.** 3 mi = _____ ft

1 foot (ft) = 12 inches

1 yard (yd) = 3 feet

1 yard (yd) = 36 inches

1 mile (mi) = 1,760 yards

1 mile (mi) = 5,280 feet

Spiral Review   (Chapter 7, Lesson 2) **KEY AF 1.2, KEY A.F 1.3**

Simplify each expression.

8. $(7 \times 8) - (42 - 6) =$ _____   **9.** $(11 - 5) \times (5 \times 4) =$ _____

10. Mrs. Duffy's class used bottle caps in an art project. Eight of the students used 12 bottle caps each. Three of the students used only 4 bottle caps each. Nine of the students used 15 bottle caps each. How many bottle caps were used by the whole class?

_____

Perimeter and Customary Units of Length

Solve each problem.

1. Grace measured the perimeter of her bedroom in feet and in yards. Which was the greater measurement: the number of feet or the number of yards? Explain your answer.

   _____

   _____

   _____

Customary Units of Length
1 foot (ft) = 12 inches (in.)
1 yard (yd) = 3 feet
1 yard (yd) = 36 inches
1 mile (mi) = 1,760 yards
1 mile (mi) = 5,280 feet

2. Grace's bedroom is 6 yards long and 12 feet wide. Find the perimeter of the room in feet. Then find the perimeter of the room in yards.

   _____

3. Grace wants to put a wallpaper border around the top of the room. Each roll of wallpaper border is 120 inches long. How many rolls will she need?

   _____

4. Grace bought material to make curtains for her bedroom windows. She bought 12 yards of material. She plans to make 6 curtains and needs 6 feet for each curtain. Did she buy enough material? Explain your answer.

   _____

   _____

   _____

5. Grace also bought 2 lengths of ribbon to trim a picture frame. One length was 18 inches. The sum of both lengths was 4 feet. What was the length of the second piece of ribbon?

   _____

6. Grace says that 9 yards is the same as 27 feet which is the same as 108 inches. What has she done wrong?

   _____

   _____

   _____

Customary Units of Capacity and Weight

CA Standard
KEY NS 3.2

Find each missing number.

16 c = _____ qt
To change from smaller units to larger units, divide by the number of cups in 1 quart.
16 ÷ 4 = 4
16 c = 4 qt

1. 4 gal = _____ pt

2. 2 pt = _____ c

3. _____ qt = 12 gal

4. _____ pt = 8 c

Customary Units of Capacity

1 pint = 2 cups
1 quart = 2 pints
1 quart = 4 cups
1 gallon = 4 quarts
1 gallon = 8 pints
1 gallon = 16 cups

Choose the unit you would use to measure the capacity of each. Write *cup, pint, quart,* or *gallon*.

5. (mug) _____

6. (Grapefruit Juice) _____

7. (barrel) _____

Compare. Write >, < or = for each ◯.

8. 4 gal ◯ 16 pt

9. 24 c ◯ 12 qt

10. 2 gal ◯ 32 cups

Spiral Review (Chapter 9, Lesson 2) **KEY** AF 1.5, AF 1.1

Complete the tables.

11. Rule: _____

Input (a)	Output
4	3
5	4
7	6

12. Rule: _____

Input (b)	Output
8	48
6	36
3	18

13. The output values in a function table are 0, 10, and 24. The rule for the table is

Output = $2m - 4$. What are the input values? _____

Customary Units of Capacity and Weight

CA Standard
KEY NS 3.2

Use the information from the table to solve each problem.

1. Jacob says that there are 64 pints in 8 gallons. Do you agree? Write a mathematical sentence that explains your answer.

_____

_____

Customary Units of Capacity

1 pint = 2 cups
1 quart = 2 pints
1 quart = 4 cups
1 gallon = 4 quarts
1 gallon = 8 pints
1 gallon = 16 cups

2. He also says that there are 34 quarts in 8 gallons. Do you agree? Write a mathematical sentence than explains your answer.

_____

3. Peggy's mother uses a pint of milk to make a milk shake. How many quarts of milk will she use to make 16 milk shakes? Write a mathematical sentence that explains your answer.

_____

_____

4. Dominic bought $\frac{1}{2}$ gallon of orange juice. Fredrick bought a six-pack of pint boxes of orange juice. Who bought more orange juice? Write a mathematical sentence that explains your answer.

_____

_____

_____

5. The ice cream shop is selling 2 1-quart containers of frozen yogurt for $3.00 and 1 gallon of frozen yogurt for $5.50. Which is the better buy? Explain your answer.

_____

_____

_____

_____

6. Tammy bought 4 gallons of frozen yogurt. Jessie bought 10 quarts of frozen yogurt. Bart bought 30 pints of frozen yogurt. Put their purchases in order from least to greatest. Explain how you solved the problem.

_____

_____

_____

_____

Metric Units of Length

CA Standards
KEY NS 3.2, **KEY** AF 1.5

Convert centimeters to decimeters.

5,000 cm = _____ dm

When you convert from smaller units to larger units the number of units decreases. So, divide by the number of centimeters in a decimeter.

5,000   ÷   10   =   500

↑   ↑   ↑

number of   centimeters in   decimeters in
centimeters   a decimeter   5,000 centimeters

Solution: 5,000 cm = 500 dm

Find the missing number.

1. 60 cm = _____ dm

2. 300 dm = _____ m

3. 4 km = _____ m

4. _____ m = 70 dm

Metric Units of Length

1 centimeter (cm) = 10 millimeters (mm)
1 decimeter (dm) = 10 centimeters
1 meter (m) = 10 decimeters
1 kilometer (km) = 1,000 meters

Complete the table. Write the rule using x and y.

5. Rule: _____

m *(x)*	10	20	30	40	50
dm *(y)*	100	200	**6.**	**7.**	**8.**

Spiral Review (Chapter 11, Lesson 3) **KEY** NS 3.2, **KEY** NS 3.3

Multiply.

9. 45 × 69 = _____   **10.** 61 × 22 = _____

11. Write a multiplication sentence with the greatest possible product using the digits 1, 2, 6, and 8 once. Then write a sentence with the least possible product.

_____

Metric Units of Length

CA Standard
KEY NS 3.2, **KEY** AF 1.5

Solve each problem.

1. What is the most reasonable metric unit to use for measuring the thickness of a DVD?

_____

Metric Units of Length
1 centimeter (cm) = 10 millimeters (mm)
1 decimeter (dm) = 10 centimeters
1 meter (m) = 10 decimeters
1 kilometer (km) = 1,000 meters

2. What is the most reasonable metric unit to use for measuring the length of a swimming pool?

_____

3. Eric ran a 5 kilometer race. How many meters did he run? Write a mathematical sentence that explains your answer.

_____

4. Ali is jogging around an exercise track in the park. The track is 200 meters long. How many times will she have to go around the track in order to jog 1 kilometer? Explain your answer.

_____

_____

5. Cara wants to make a stack of encyclopedias that will be 1 meter high. Each book is 5 centimeters wide. How many books will she need? Explain your answer.

_____

6. May Alice rode her bike 3 kilometers. Darren rode his bike 4,000 meters. Gary rode his bike 10,000 decimeters. Who rode the longest distance?

_____

_____

Metric Units of Capacity and Mass

CA Standards
KEY NS 3.2, MR 3.2

Find each missing number.

9 L = _____ mL
To change from larger units to smaller units, multiply by the number of milliliters in 1 liter.
$9 \times 1,000 = 9,000$
9 L = 9,000 mL

Metric Units of Capacity
1 liter = 1,000 milliliters

1. 17,000 mL = _____ L   **2.** _____ mL = 16 L

3. 41 L = _____ mL   **4.** _____ L = 10,000 mL

Choose the better estimate of capacity of each.

5.   **a.** 2 mL   **b.** 2 L

6. WATER   **a.** 500 mL   **b.** 50 L

7.   **a.** 400 mL   **b.** 4 L

Choose the better unit to measure each capacity.
Write *milliliters* or *liters*.

8. an eyedropper   **9.** a large pitcher   **10.** a spoon

_____   _____   _____

Spiral Review   (Chapter 11, Lesson 4) **KEY** NS 3.2, **KEY** NS 3.3

Multiply.

11. $234 \times 52 =$ _____   **12.** $406 \times 43 =$ _____

13. Mary's class collected cans for recycling. They put 2 dozen cans in each sack. They had 104 sacks at the end of the year. How many cans did they collect?

_____

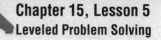
Metric Units of Capacity and Mass

Solve each problem.

Metric Units of Capacity
1 liter (L) = 1,000 milliliters (mL)

Metric Units of Mass
1 kilogram (kg) = 1,000 grams (g)

1. A box of hot cocoa packets has 30 grams of hot cocoa mix. How many boxes of mix can be made from 6 kilograms of hot cocoa mix?

_____

2. A serving of chicken noodle soup is 120 mL. How many liters of soup will the cafeteria need to serve 350 students?

_____

3. A serving of green beans is 125 g. The cafeteria has 10 5-kilogram cans of green beans. Does the cafeteria have enough green beans to serve 350 students? Show your work.

_____
_____
_____
_____
_____

4. A granola bar weighs 30 g. 100 granola bars are in a shipping carton. How many kilograms do a dozen shipping cartons weigh? Show your work.

_____
_____
_____
_____
_____

5. A serving of juice is 250 mL. How many servings are in a dozen liters of juice? Show your work.

_____
_____
_____
_____

6. Mrs. Franks bought 6 large jugs of milk. A large jug holds 4 liters of milk. A serving size is 250 mL. If each of the 4 people in Mrs. Franks' family has 2 servings of milk a day, will the 6 jugs be enough milk for one week? Show your work.

_____
_____
_____
_____
_____

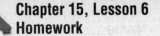

Problem Solving: Estimated or Exact Amounts

CA Standards
KEY NS 3.1, NS 2.1

Solve. Explain why you used estimates or exact numbers.

The Burlington Elementary School had a general assembly of all students at the school. The students were seated according to what grade they were in. The table shows how many students attended from each grade.

Student Assembly	
Grade	Number of Students
1	116
2	98
3	162
4	139

How many more fourth-grade students than second-grade students attended the assembly?

Step ❶

Decide what kind of answer you need. The question asks "how many more." You need an exact answer.

Step ❷

Decide what operation you need to do. The question asks "how many more." You need to subtract.

$139 - 98 = 41$

Solution: 41 more fourth-grade students than second-grade students attended the assembly.

1. About how many students attended the general assembly altogether?

   _____

   _____

2. The first and second graders sat together in the general assembly. About how many students were there in this group?

   _____

   _____

3. After the first half of the assembly, the first-graders were sent back to class. How many students were left attending the general assembly?

   _____

   _____

Problem Solving: Estimated or Exact Amounts

Solve each problem. Explain why you used estimates or exact numbers.

1. Ashley, Drew, and Karen are counselors at a summer camp. Drew drove 149 miles to Ashley's house, picked her up, and then they drove together another 215 miles to the camp. About how many miles did Drew drive?

_____

_____

_____

2. Last year at the camp, there were 324 boys and 335 girls. How many more girls than boys were there?

_____

_____

_____

3. Last year there were 142 counselors at the camp. How many more campers were there than counselors?

_____

_____

_____

4. The counselors divide the campers into equal groups each with one counselor. About how many campers are assigned to each counselor?

_____

_____

_____

5. Each morning activity at the camp is 45 minutes long. If there are 4 activity sessions, how many hours of activities do the campers have before lunchtime?

_____

_____

_____

6. In the afternoons, campers can participate in four activities for 2 hours before rest time. Of the 659 campers, 60 went horseback riding, 127 did arts and crafts, and 82 practiced archery. The rest participated in swimming in the lake. How many campers went swimming?

_____

_____

_____

Hands On: Negative Numbers on the Number Line

Negative numbers are to the left of 0 on the number line. Positive numbers are to the right of 0. What are the integers for Points *A* and *B*?

```
            A                   B
◄─┼──┼──┼──┼──┼──┼──┼──┼──┼──┼──┼──┼──┼──┼──┼──┼──┼──┼──┼──┼──►
 ⁻10⁻9⁻8⁻7⁻6⁻5⁻4⁻3⁻2⁻1  0  1  2  3  4  5  6  7  8  9 10
```

Solution: *A* is at ⁻5. *B* is at 4.

Write the integer for the letter on the number line.

```
   A    B  C        D    E   F    G H    I         J
◄─┼──┼──┼──┼──┼──┼──┼──┼──┼──┼──┼──┼──┼──┼──┼──┼──┼──┼──┼──┼──►
 ⁻10⁻9⁻8⁻7⁻6⁻5⁻4⁻3⁻2⁻1  0  1  2  3  4  5  6  7  8  9 10
```

1. B _____   **2.** G _____   **3.** C _____   **4.** J _____

5. D _____   **6.** A _____   **7.** H _____   **8.** I _____

Spiral Review (Chapter 14, Lessons 2, 3) NS 4.0, **KEY** NS 4.2, NS 4.1

9. What are the factors of 6?

10. Is 9 a prime or a composite number?

_____   _____

11. Thomas has 6 pieces of candy. If he wanted to split the pieces of candy up into equal groups, what are the different ways that he could do it?

_____

_____

Hands On: Negative Numbers on the Number Line

Solve each problem. You can make a number line to help you. Write your answers as positive or negative numbers.

1. You are at street level (0). You go up 6 floors, then you go down 10 floors. Where are you now?

_____

2. You are in the basement, 3 floors below street level. You go down 5 floors, then you go up 11 floors. Where are you?

_____

3. You are 2 floors above street level. You go down 3 floors and up 1 floor. You go down 3 floors and up 1 floor again. You go down 3 floors and up 1 floor a third time. Where are you?

_____

4. You are 15 floors below street level. You go up 10 floors, and up 10 more floors. Then you go down 5 floors. Where are you?

_____

For Problems 5 and 6, north and east are positive. South and west are negative.

5. Your school is at 0. After school, you walk 7 blocks south to the basketball court. After the game, you walk 8 blocks south to a friend's house. Later you take the bus 26 blocks north to your home. Where are you?

_____

6. Your home is at 0. You walk east 6 blocks to the library—but you left your library card at home! You walk west 6 blocks to your home, get your card, and walk 6 blocks east again to the library. Then you walk 10 blocks west to the park. You and your friends walk 4 blocks west to get pizza. Where are you?

_____

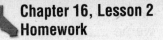
Compare Positive and Negative Numbers

CA Standards
KEY NS 1.8, NS 1.0

Which is greater, ⁻6 or ⁻1?

The number farther to the right on the number line has the greater value.

```
←―+――+――+――+――+――+――+――+――+――+――+――+――+――+――+――+――→
  ⁻8 ⁻7 ⁻6 ⁻5 ⁻4 ⁻3 ⁻2 ⁻1  0  1  2  3  4  5  6  7  8
```

Solution: ⁻1 is greater than ⁻6. ⁻1 > ⁻6.

Use the number line and the symbols >, <, or = to complete the number ⁻1 sentence.

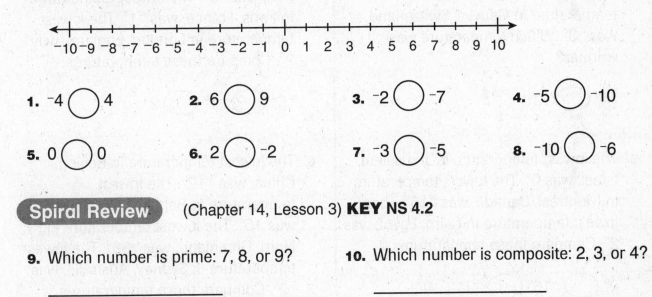

```
←―+――+――+――+――+――+――+――+――+――+――+――+――+――+――+――+――+――+――+――+――+――→
 ⁻10 ⁻9 ⁻8 ⁻7 ⁻6 ⁻5 ⁻4 ⁻3 ⁻2 ⁻1  0  1  2  3  4  5  6  7  8  9  10
```

1. ⁻4 ◯ 4   **2.** 6 ◯ 9   **3.** ⁻2 ◯ ⁻7   **4.** ⁻5 ◯ ⁻10

5. 0 ◯ 0   **6.** 2 ◯ ⁻2   **7.** ⁻3 ◯ ⁻5   **8.** ⁻10 ◯ ⁻6

Spiral Review   (Chapter 14, Lesson 3) **KEY NS 4.2**

9. Which number is prime: 7, 8, or 9?   **10.** Which number is composite: 2, 3, or 4?

_____   _____

11. Marcia likes prime numbers! For breakfast, she ate 2 eggs and
3 pieces of bacon. How many orange slices could she have eaten?
(The number is more than 3.)

_____

Use with text pp. 350–351

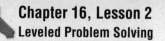
Compare Positive and Negative Numbers

CA Standards
KEY NS 1.8, NS 1.0

Use the symbols >, <, or = to complete the number sentence.

1. The lowest temperature in Budapest, Hungary, was 10°. The lowest temperature in Shanghai, China, was ⁻10°. Which temperature was warmer?

   10° ◯ ⁻10°

2. The lowest temperature in Stockholm, Sweden, was ⁻26°. The lowest temperature in Toronto, Canada, was ⁻26°. Which temperature was warmer?

   ⁻26° ◯ ⁻26°

3. The lowest temperature in Berlin, Germany, was ⁻4°. The lowest temperature in Geneva, Switzerland, was ⁻3°. Which temperature was warmer?

   ⁻4° ◯ ⁻3°

4. The lowest temperature in Tehran, Iran, was ⁻5°. The lowest temperature in Paris, France, was ⁻1°. The lowest temperature in London, England, was 2°. Compare these temperatures.

   ⁻5° ◯ ⁻1° ◯ 2°

5. The lowest temperature in Jerusalem, Israel, was 0°. The lowest temperature in Montreal, Canada, was ⁻16°. The lowest temperature in Cairo, Egypt, was 2°. Compare these temperatures.

   0° ◯ ⁻16° ◯ ⁻2°

6. The lowest temperature in Beijing, China, was ⁻12°. The lowest temperature in Bangkok, Thailand, was 15°. The lowest temperature in Nord, Greenland, was ⁻36°. The lowest temperature in Sydney, Australia, was ⁻9°. Compare these temperatures.

   ⁻12° ◯ ⁻15° ◯ ⁻36° ◯ ⁻9°

Use Negative Numbers

CA Standards
KEY NS 1.8, NS 1.0

You can use a number line to help you solve problems.

You owe your brother $7. You pay back $2. How much do you owe him now?

$$\leftarrow\!\!\mid\!\!+\!\!+\!\!\blacklozenge\!\!+\!\!+\!\!+\!\!+\!\!\blacklozenge\!\!\mid\!\!+\!\!+\!\!+\!\!+\!\!+\!\!+\!\!+\!\!+\!\!\mid\!\!\rightarrow$$

‾8 ‾7 ‾6 ‾5 ‾4 ‾3 ‾2 ‾1 0 1 2 3 4 5 6 7 8

Solution: You owe $5 now.

Use the number line to help you find the amount.

‾10 ‾9 ‾8 ‾7 ‾6 ‾5 ‾4 ‾3 ‾2 ‾1 0 1 2 3 4 5 6 7 8 9 10

1. 3 more than ‾5   **2.** 8 more than 0   **3.** 7 fewer than 4   **4.** 5 fewer than 8

_____   _____   _____   _____

5. 9 fewer than 9   **6.** 4 fewer than 0   **7.** 2 more than ‾1   **8.** 3 fewer than ‾6

_____   _____   _____   _____

Spiral Review   (Chapter 15, Lesson 2) **KEY** NS 3.2

Find the missing number.

9. 6 yards = _____ feet   **10.** 4 feet = _____ inches

11. Greg has a rope 6 yards long. How many inches long is the rope?

_____

Use Negative Numbers

CA Standards
KEY NS 1.8, NS 1.0

Solve each problem.

1. You owed your friend $15. You paid back $8. How much do you owe now?

_____

2. Your friend owed you $10. She paid back $6. How much does she owe you now?

_____

3. You borrowed $26 from your friend. You paid back $5 and then you paid back $4 more. How much do you owe now?

_____

4. Your friend borrowed $18 from you. He paid back $3. Then he borrowed $5 more. How much does he owe you now?

_____

5. You borrowed $30 from your mother. The next week, you paid back $10. A week later, you borrowed $4. A week after that, you paid back $12. How much do you still owe your mother?

_____

6. You lent your sister $10. She paid back $2 a week for 4 weeks. Then she borrowed $7. She paid back $8. She says she doesn't owe you any more money. Is she correct?

_____

Name _____ Date _____

Hands On: Model Fractions

CA Standards
NS 1.5, NS 1.7

Write a fraction for the shaded part. Then write a fraction for the part that is not shaded.

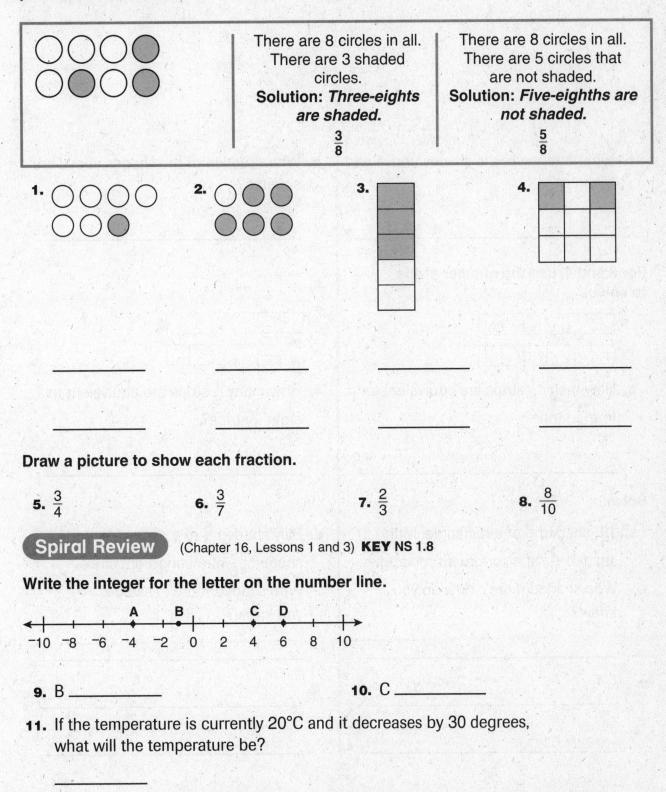

There are 8 circles in all. There are 3 shaded circles.
Solution: *Three-eights are shaded.*
$\frac{3}{8}$

There are 8 circles in all. There are 5 circles that are not shaded.
Solution: *Five-eighths are not shaded.*
$\frac{5}{8}$

1.

2.

3.

4.

_____   _____   _____   _____

_____   _____   _____   _____

Draw a picture to show each fraction.

5. $\frac{3}{4}$

6. $\frac{3}{7}$

7. $\frac{2}{3}$

8. $\frac{8}{10}$

Spiral Review   (Chapter 16, Lessons 1 and 3) **KEY** NS 1.8

Write the integer for the letter on the number line.

9. B _____

10. C _____

11. If the temperature is currently 20°C and it decreases by 30 degrees, what will the temperature be?

_____

Hands On: Model Fractions

For 1 and 2, use the diagram to solve.

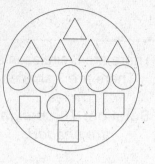

1. What fraction of the shapes above are triangles?

_____

2. What fraction of the shapes above are squares?

_____

For 3 and 4, use the number strips to solve.

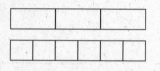

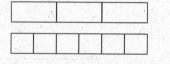

3. How many $\frac{1}{3}$ strips are equivalent to four $\frac{1}{6}$ strips?

_____

4. How many $\frac{1}{6}$ strips are equivalent to eight $\frac{1}{3}$ strips?

_____

Solve.

5. J.T. shaded $\frac{3}{5}$ of a rectangle. Mary shaded $\frac{4}{12}$ of a congruent rectangle. Who shaded more? How do you know?

_____

_____

_____

6. Billy shaded $\frac{6}{8}$ of a circle. Mary shaded $\frac{15}{16}$ of a congruent circle. Who shaded more? How do you know?

_____

_____

_____

Fractional Parts of a Number

CA Standard
NS 1.5

Find the fractional part of each number.

$\frac{2}{3}$ of 12

Divide to find the number in each group.

$12 \div 3 = 4$

Multiply by the number of groups.

$4 \times 2 = 8$

Solution:

$\frac{2}{3}$ of 12 = 8

1. $\frac{2}{3}$ of 6 = _____

2. $\frac{3}{8}$ of 24 = _____

3. $\frac{2}{5}$ of 25 = _____

4. $\frac{3}{10}$ of 50 = _____

5. $\frac{4}{7}$ of 35 = _____

6. $\frac{3}{4}$ of 36 = _____

7. $\frac{1}{4}$ of 32 = _____

8. $\frac{2}{11}$ of 44 = _____

9. $\frac{3}{5}$ of 45 = _____

10. $\frac{5}{9}$ of 27 = _____

11. $\frac{5}{8}$ of 64 = _____

12. $\frac{7}{10}$ of 80 = _____

13. $\frac{11}{15}$ of 45 = _____

14. $\frac{3}{20}$ of 120 = _____

15. $\frac{2}{3}$ of 42 = _____

16. $\frac{1}{8}$ of 40 = _____

Spiral Review (Chapter 14, Lesson 4) **KEY** NS 4.2, NS 4.1

Make a factor tree for each number.

17. 45

18. 30

_____

_____

_____

_____

_____

_____

19. The factor tree for 60 has all of the factors in the factor trees for 15 and 30, but not 45. Explain why this is true.

_____

_____

Fractional Parts of a Number

Solve.

1. Justin has 20 CD's. If one-half of the CD's are hip-hop, how many CD's are hip-hop?

   _____

2. Marianna has 15 apples. If one-third of the apples are Granny Smith, how many Granny Smiths does she have?

   _____

3. Leah lives in an apartment building with 100 apartments. One-fifth of the apartments have one bedroom, two-fifths are apartments that have two bedrooms, and the rest have three bedroms. How many three-bedroom apartments are in the building?

   _____

4. Analee has 30 gumballs. If one-sixth are green, and one-third are red, are there more red gumballs or green gumballs? How do you know?

   _____

   _____

   _____

   _____

5. Aldin scored two-thirds of the baskets in a basketball game. If 60 total baskets were scored, how many did Aldin score?

   _____

6. Malcom has 200 coins. If one-fourth of the coins are dimes and one-tenth of the remaining coins are pennies, how many pennies does Malcom have?

   _____

Name _____ Date _____

Hands On: Model Equivalent Fractions   CA Standards
NS 1.7, KEY NS 1.9

$\frac{4}{12}$ and $\frac{2}{6}$

Use fraction strips to show $\frac{4}{12}$ and $\frac{2}{6}$.

Solution:

Yes, $\frac{4}{12}$ and $\frac{2}{6}$ are equivalent fractions.

1					
$\frac{1}{6}$	$\frac{1}{6}$				
$\frac{1}{12}$ $\frac{1}{12}$ $\frac{1}{12}$ $\frac{1}{12}$					

**Decide whether the fractions are equivalent. Write yes or no.
Use fraction strips to help you.**

1. $\frac{3}{12}$ and $\frac{1}{4}$ 2. $\frac{3}{6}$ and $\frac{1}{3}$ 3. $\frac{2}{5}$ and $\frac{4}{10}$ 4. $\frac{3}{3}$ and $\frac{5}{5}$

_____   _____   _____   _____

**Find a fraction equivalent to each. Draw number
lines to help you.**

5. $\frac{1}{5}$ 6. $\frac{4}{8}$ 7. $\frac{6}{10}$ 8. $\frac{8}{10}$ 9. $\frac{7}{8}$ 10. $\frac{4}{5}$

_____   _____   _____   _____   _____   _____

Spiral Review   (Chapter 15, Lesson 3) **KEY** NS 3.2

Find the missing number.

11. 10 gallons = _____ pints   12. 15 pounds = _____ ounces

13. Kevin has a box that weighs 20 pounds. Marlena has a box that weighs 300 ounces.
Which box is heavier? How do you know?

_____

_____

_____

Name _____ Date _____

Hands On: Model Equivalent Fractions

CA Standards
NS 1.7, **KEY** NS 1.9

Solve. Draw number lines or fraction strips to help you.

1. Mary-Lou ate 2 out of 8 slices from a pizza pie. What two fractions show how much of the pie she ate?

_____

2. James and Ahn-Lee shared a taxi fare. James paid one-third of the fare and Ahn-Lee paid two-fifths of the fare. Did they pay the same amount?

_____

_____

3. Lev ate one-third of a birthday cake. He claims he ate more than Liana, who ate one-fifth of the cake. Liana says that she ate more because 5 is larger than 3. Who ate more? Explain how you know.

_____

_____

4. Frank and Maxine are comparing the number of boys and girls in the class. Frank says there are 12 boys out of a total of 24 students. Maxine says there is 1 boy for every 2 students. Are the two responses the same? Explain how you know.

_____

_____

5. Han ate 3 apples out of a bag of 6 apples. Lester ate 2 apples out of a bag of 5 apples. Use equivalent fractions to decide if Han or Lester ate a larger part of the total apples from each bag. Explain your answer.

_____

_____

6. Bea ate 2 donuts out of a box of 12 donuts. Bella ate 1 donut out of a box of 6 donuts. Use equivalent fractions to decide if Bea or Bella ate a larger part of the total donuts from each box. Explain your answer.

_____

_____

Name _____ Date _____

Equivalent Fractions

CA Standards
NS 1.5, KEY NS 1.9

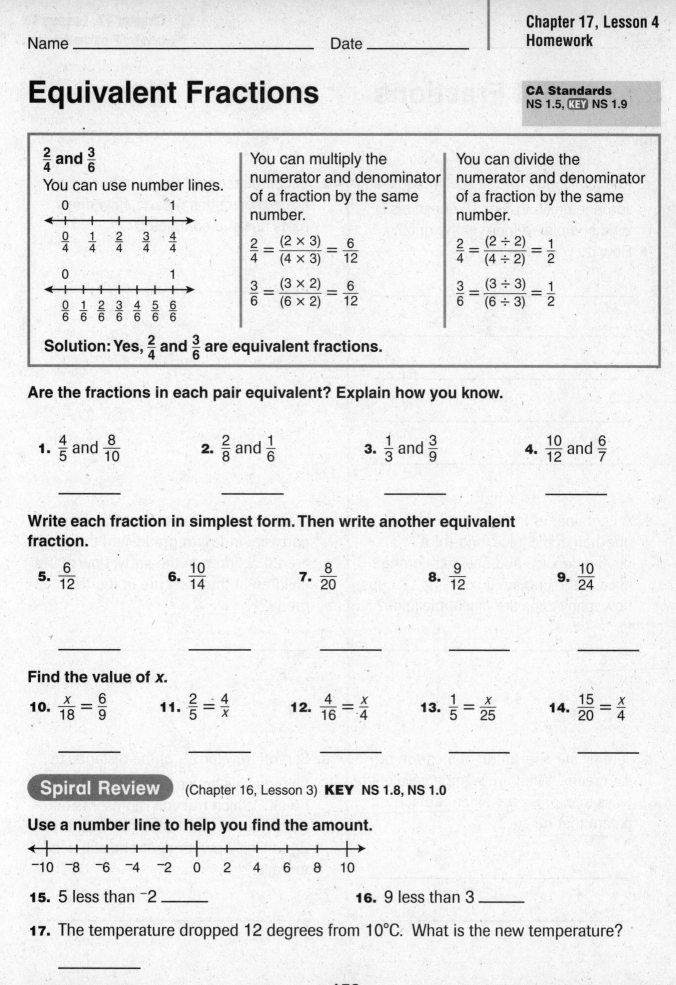

$\frac{2}{4}$ and $\frac{3}{6}$

You can use number lines.

You can multiply the numerator and denominator of a fraction by the same number.

$$\frac{2}{4} = \frac{(2 \times 3)}{(4 \times 3)} = \frac{6}{12}$$

$$\frac{3}{6} = \frac{(3 \times 2)}{(6 \times 2)} = \frac{6}{12}$$

You can divide the numerator and denominator of a fraction by the same number.

$$\frac{2}{4} = \frac{(2 \div 2)}{(4 \div 2)} = \frac{1}{2}$$

$$\frac{3}{6} = \frac{(3 \div 3)}{(6 \div 3)} = \frac{1}{2}$$

Solution: Yes, $\frac{2}{4}$ and $\frac{3}{6}$ are equivalent fractions.

Are the fractions in each pair equivalent? Explain how you know.

1. $\frac{4}{5}$ and $\frac{8}{10}$

2. $\frac{2}{8}$ and $\frac{1}{6}$

3. $\frac{1}{3}$ and $\frac{3}{9}$

4. $\frac{10}{12}$ and $\frac{6}{7}$

_____ _____ _____ _____

Write each fraction in simplest form. Then write another equivalent fraction.

5. $\frac{6}{12}$

6. $\frac{10}{14}$

7. $\frac{8}{20}$

8. $\frac{9}{12}$

9. $\frac{10}{24}$

_____ _____ _____ _____ _____

Find the value of x.

10. $\frac{x}{18} = \frac{6}{9}$

11. $\frac{2}{5} = \frac{4}{x}$

12. $\frac{4}{16} = \frac{x}{4}$

13. $\frac{1}{5} = \frac{x}{25}$

14. $\frac{15}{20} = \frac{x}{4}$

_____ _____ _____ _____ _____

Spiral Review (Chapter 16, Lesson 3) **KEY** NS 1.8, NS 1.0

Use a number line to help you find the amount.

$^-$10 $^-$8 $^-$6 $^-$4 $^-$2 0 2 4 6 8 10

15. 5 less than $^-$2 _____

16. 9 less than 3 _____

17. The temperature dropped 12 degrees from 10°C. What is the new temperature?

_____

Equivalent Fractions

Solve.

1. Kami finished $\frac{1}{2}$ of the spelling quiz and Jordana finished 5 of 10 questions. Who completed more of the quiz? How do you know?

   _____

   _____

   _____

   _____

2. Vi completed two-thirds of her project. If the project has 6 parts, how many parts has she completed?

   _____

3. A container of fruit punch contains one-half apple juice, one-third pineapple juice and one-sixth orange juice. If the container contains 12 cups, how many cups are pineapple juice?

   _____

4. If one-fourth of the children at Trina's party are in fourth grade, and there are 20 children at the party, how many children at the party are in fourth grade?

   _____

5. Jeremy ate one-fourth of a carton of ice cream. What are some equivalent ways to express the amount of ice cream that he ate?

   _____

6. Samriti traveled $\frac{7}{12}$ of the distance to her cousin's house before taking a break. Which fraction represents the remainder of her trip? If her total trip is 240 miles, how far does she still need to travel?

   _____

Name _____ Date _____

Add and Subtract Fractions

CA Standard
NS 1.5

Add or subtract. Write your answer in simplest form.

$\frac{3}{8} + \frac{1}{8}$

Add the numerators. Keep the denominator the same.

$\frac{3}{8} + \frac{1}{8} = \frac{4}{8}$

Write the answer in simplest form.

$\frac{4}{8} = \frac{(4 \div 4)}{(8 \div 4)} = \frac{1}{2}$

Solution:

$\frac{3}{8} + \frac{1}{8} = \frac{1}{2}$

1. $\frac{2}{6} + \frac{2}{6} =$

_____

3. $\frac{5}{8} + \frac{3}{8} =$

_____

2. $\frac{4}{7} - \frac{2}{7} =$

_____

4. $\frac{6}{8} - \frac{2}{8} =$

_____

5. $\frac{1}{7} + \frac{5}{7} =$

_____

6. $\frac{8}{12} + \frac{2}{12} =$

_____

7. $\frac{6}{9} + \frac{2}{9} =$

_____

8. $\frac{8}{12} - \frac{4}{12} =$

_____

Find the value of n.

9. $\frac{6}{10} - \frac{n}{10} = \frac{3}{10}$

_____

10. $\frac{n}{9} + \frac{5}{9} = \frac{8}{9}$

_____

11. $\frac{7}{8} - \frac{n}{8} = \frac{4}{8}$

_____

Spiral Review (Chapter 10, Lesson 2) **KEY** NS 1.4, MR 2.5

12. Estimate 7 × 98 _____

13. Estimate 41 × 6,939 _____

14. Jai has 5 bags of candy with 43 pieces in each bag. He estimates that he has about 250 pieces of candy. Is this a reasonable estimate? Explain.

_____

Add and Subtract Fractions

Solve.

1. Basia ate one-fifth of a cake and Karolina ate two-fifths of the cake. How much of the cake did the girls eat together?

_____

2. Luis walked one-eighth of the distance to school. What part of the distance to school does he still need to walk?

_____

3. Johnny wants to buy a game system. If his dad agrees to pay six-sevenths of the cost of the game system, what fraction of the cost will Johnny pay?

_____

4. Tony filled one-fourth of a bowl with water. He then filled an additional one-half of the bowl. What portion of the bowl is filled with water?

_____

5. Marnie completed one-fifth of her homework assignment right after school. She completed two-fifths of the assignment after dinner. How much of the assignment does she still need to complete?

_____

6. Chris planted one-sixth of his watermelon seeds and 20 cucumber seeds. If he planted 26 seeds total, how many watermelon seeds does he have left?

_____

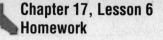
Problem Solving:
Use a Simpler Problem

CA Standards
MR 2.2, NS 1.5

Tobias and Kelly both use chocolate chips when baking cookies. Tobias uses $\frac{7}{12}$ of a bag of chocolate chips. Kelly uses $\frac{5}{12}$ of a bag. How much more of a bag of chips does Tobias use?

What you know: Tobias uses $\frac{7}{12}$ of a bag of chocolate chips.

Kelly uses $\frac{5}{12}$ of a bag of chocolate chips.

Use easier numbers to solve the problem.

What if Tobias used 7 bags and Kelly used 5 bags? Subtract $7 - 5 = 2$.
Reread the problem. Solve using original numbers.
Subtract.

$\frac{7}{12} - \frac{5}{12} = \frac{2}{12}$

So Tobias used $\frac{2}{12}$ more of the bag than Kelly.

Use a simpler problem to solve. Explain why it makes sense.

1. Jenny's water glass is $\frac{3}{4}$ full and Maggie's glass is $\frac{1}{4}$ full. How much

   more full is Jenny's glass? _____

2. Brian has a recipe that calls for $\frac{5}{8}$ cup of flour. He has $\frac{3}{8}$ cup. How

   many more cups does he need? _____

3. Juan has $\frac{3}{8}$ cup of sugar. Marisol has $\frac{2}{8}$ cup of sugar. How many

   cups of sugar do they have together? _____

Spiral Review (Chapter 16, Lesson 1) **KEY NS 1.8**

Write the integer for the situation.

4. Eighteen feet below sea level.

5. Fifty degrees below zero.

Problem Solving:
Use a Simpler Problem

1. Kayla has $\frac{1}{5}$ container of animal crackers. Jessi has $\frac{3}{5}$ container of animal crackers. If they combine their animal crackers, what fraction of a container do Kayla and Jessi have together?

   _____

2. Maura spent $\frac{2}{3}$ of her recess on the jungle gym. What fractional part of her recess time does she have remaining?

   _____

3. Dashawn and Darnell shared a birthday cake. Dashawn ate $\frac{3}{14}$ of the cake and Darnell ate $\frac{4}{14}$ of the cake. What fraction of the cake did they eat together?

   _____

4. Mr. Tsourounis' law firm moved into a new office. On Monday, $\frac{3}{14}$ of the office was moved. If the remainder was moved on Tuesday, what fraction of the office was moved on Tuesday?

   _____

5. Benny went to the store to buy vegetables, cereal and milk. He spent $\frac{4}{9}$ of his money on vegetables and $\frac{2}{9}$ of his money on cereal. What fraction of his money did he spend on milk?

   _____

6. Alex used $\frac{4}{13}$ of his allowance to buy ice cream and $\frac{7}{13}$ of his allowance to go to the movies. What fraction of his allowance does he have left?

   _____

Hands On: Compare Fractions

CA Standard
KEY NS 1.9

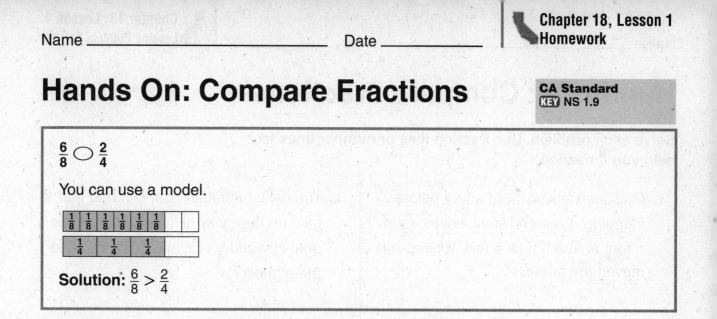

$\frac{6}{8} \bigcirc \frac{2}{4}$

You can use a model.

| $\frac{1}{8}$ | $\frac{1}{8}$ | $\frac{1}{8}$ | $\frac{1}{8}$ | $\frac{1}{8}$ | $\frac{1}{8}$ | | |

| $\frac{1}{4}$ | $\frac{1}{4}$ | $\frac{1}{4}$ | |

Solution: $\frac{6}{8} > \frac{2}{4}$

Compare. Write >, <, or = for each ◯. Use fraction tiles or number lines to help you.

1. $\frac{5}{10} \bigcirc \frac{2}{4}$ **2.** $\frac{2}{3} \bigcirc \frac{7}{9}$ **3.** $\frac{1}{4} \bigcirc \frac{3}{4}$ **4.** $\frac{3}{8} \bigcirc \frac{6}{16}$

_____   _____   _____   _____

5. $\frac{4}{5} \bigcirc \frac{2}{5}$ **6.** $\frac{3}{6} \bigcirc \frac{4}{8}$ **7.** $\frac{3}{9} \bigcirc \frac{3}{10}$ **8.** $\frac{3}{7} \bigcirc \frac{5}{7}$

_____   _____   _____   _____

Spiral Review   (Chapter 13, Lessons 2, 4) **KEY** NS 3.0, **KEY** NS 3.4

Divide. Use multiplication to check.

9. $420 \div 4$ _____   **10.** $622 \div 2$ _____

11. A restaurant served 410 people on Saturday and Sunday. If the same number of people ate there each day, how many were served on Saturday? _____

Hands On: Compare Fractions

CA Standard
KEY NS 1.9

Solve each problem. Use fraction tiles or number lines to help you if needed.

1. One snail moved $\frac{4}{12}$ of a foot before stopping. A second snail moved $\frac{6}{12}$ of a foot before it took a rest. Which snail moved the farthest?

_____

2. The male mountain goat climbed $\frac{3}{4}$ of a mile up the rocky cliff side. The female goat climbed $\frac{1}{4}$ of a mile. Who climbed the highest?

_____

3. Jerry swam $\frac{1}{3}$ of a mile across the lake and rested on a raft. Then he swam another $\frac{2}{6}$ of a mile to the opposite shore. Did he swim more, less, or the same distance before he rested than after he rested?

_____

_____

4. Tomas ran $\frac{1}{2}$ of a mile around the track. Wendy ran $\frac{3}{4}$ of a mile around the track. Who ran the farthest?

_____

5. Three friends shared a pizza. Paul ate $\frac{1}{8}$ of the pizza. Abe ate $\frac{2}{4}$ and Carrie ate $\frac{3}{8}$. Who ate the most? Who ate the least?

_____

6. Three friends drove to a national park to go hiking. They decided to share the driving. Moritz drove $\frac{3}{5}$ of the way. Pablo drove $\frac{3}{10}$ of the way and Reggie drove $\frac{2}{20}$ of the way. Who drove the greatest distance? Who drove the least distance?

_____

Use with text pp. 392–393

Compare and Order Fractions

CA Standards
KEY NS 1.9, NS 1.5

Compare $\frac{6}{8}$ and $\frac{2}{4}$.

$\frac{6}{8}$ ◯ $\frac{2}{4}$.

Way 1 You can use a model.

| $\frac{1}{8}$ | $\frac{1}{8}$ | $\frac{1}{8}$ | $\frac{1}{8}$ | $\frac{1}{8}$ | $\frac{1}{8}$ | |
| $\frac{1}{4}$ | | $\frac{1}{4}$ | | | | |

$\frac{6}{8} > \frac{2}{4}$

Way 2 You can use equivalent fractions.

$\frac{2}{4} = \frac{(2 \times 2)}{(4 \times 2)} = \frac{4}{8}$

$\frac{6}{8}$ is greater than $\frac{4}{8}$, so

Solution: $\frac{6}{8} > \frac{2}{4}$

Compare. Write >, <, or = for each ◯.

1. $\frac{5}{10}$ ◯ $\frac{2}{4}$ _____

2. $\frac{2}{3}$ ◯ $\frac{7}{9}$ _____

3. $\frac{1}{4}$ ◯ $\frac{4}{8}$ _____

4. $\frac{3}{8}$ ◯ $\frac{6}{16}$ _____

5. $\frac{5}{5}$ ◯ $\frac{4}{5}$ _____

6. $\frac{3}{6}$ ◯ $\frac{4}{8}$ _____

7. $\frac{3}{9}$ ◯ $\frac{3}{10}$ _____

8. $\frac{7}{7}$ ◯ $\frac{4}{4}$ _____

Order the fractions from least to greatest. Use number lines to help you.

9. $\frac{1}{5}, \frac{4}{5}, \frac{3}{5}$

10. $\frac{3}{6}, \frac{5}{6}, \frac{4}{6}$

11. $\frac{5}{9}, \frac{2}{3}, \frac{7}{9}$

12. $\frac{4}{8}, \frac{7}{16}, \frac{9}{16}$

_____ _____ _____ _____

Spiral Review (Chapter 13, Lessons 2, 3, 4) **KEY NS 3.0, KEY NS 3.2, KEY NS 3.4**

Divide. Use multiplication to check.

13. $486 \div 3$ _____

14. $864 \div 2$ _____

15. Five trucks carried 250 tons of coal. If the trucks each carried the same load, how many tons of coal did each have? _____

Compare and Order Fractions

CA Standards
KEY NS 1.9, NS 1.5

Solve each problem.

1. Edie, George, and Art dug holes to plant seedlings. Edie dug $\frac{2}{4}$ feet. George's hole was $\frac{3}{4}$ feet deep and Art's was $\frac{1}{4}$ feet deep. Order the fractions from least to greatest.

_____

2. Edie's seedling was $\frac{3}{5}$ feet in length. Art's was $\frac{2}{5}$ feet long and George's was $\frac{4}{5}$ feet tall. Who planted the tallest seedling? The shortest seedling?

_____

3. The weather was very hot and the students watered their seedlings daily. Art poured $\frac{1}{2}$ gallon of water on his seedling. Edie poured $\frac{3}{10}$ of a gallon on hers. George watered his seedling with $\frac{6}{10}$ of a gallon. Order the fractions from greatest to least.

_____

4. Hank's vegetable garden covers $\frac{3}{6}$ of an acre. Polly's garden is $\frac{1}{3}$ of an acre and Estella's is $\frac{5}{6}$ of an acre. Whose garden is the largest? Whose is the smallest?

_____

5. Estella has divided her garden into three sections. The section where she grows tomatoes takes up $\frac{2}{6}$ of the garden. She plants $\frac{1}{4}$ of the garden with beans. Corn is in the remaining $\frac{5}{12}$. Order the vegetables by the space they use from greatest to least.

_____

_____

6. Hank's biggest tomato weighs $\frac{2}{5}$ of a pound. Estella's largest tomato weighs $\frac{7}{20}$ of a pound, while Polly's largest weighs in at $\frac{3}{10}$ pound. Order the tomatoes by owner from least to greatest weight.

_____

_____

Use with text pp. 394–397

Name _____ Date _____

Write Mixed Numbers and Improper Fractions

CA Standards
KEY NS 1.9, NS 1.7

Write an improper fraction and a mixed number to describe the shaded part.

Step 1 There are 3 whole squares and $\frac{2}{5}$ of the fourth square is shaded.

Step 2 $\frac{5}{5} + \frac{5}{5} + \frac{5}{5} + \frac{2}{5} = \frac{17}{5}$

Step 3 $1 + 1 + 1 + \frac{2}{5} = 3\frac{2}{5}$

Solution: $3\frac{2}{5}$ and $\frac{17}{5}$

Write an improper fraction and a mixed number or whole number to describe the shaded parts.

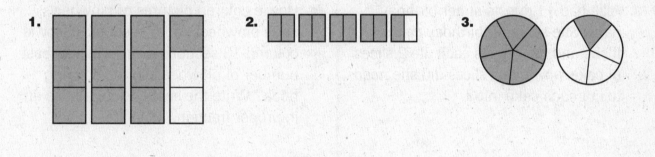

1. _____

2. _____

3. _____

Spiral Review (Chapter 15, Lesson 4) **KEY** NS 3.2

Find the missing number.

4. 200 mm = _____ cm

5. 3,000 m = _____ km

6. A building is 6 meters high. What is its height in centimeters? _____

Write Mixed Numbers and Improper Fractions

Solve each problem.

1. Jerry bought 2 pies. He cut each pie into 6 slices. Over a week, he ate all of one pie and 2 slices of the second. How much of the total number of slices did he eat? Write your answer as an improper fraction.

   _____

2. Ms. Rodriguez had 2 boxes of chalk at the start of the school year. Each box contained 10 pieces of chalk. By the end of the school year, she had used all of the chalk in one box and half of the other. How much of the chalk did she use? Write your answer as a mixed number.

   _____

3. Allie had 11 guests at her birthday party. She served 2 birthday cakes. If she and her guests each ate 2 slices of cake, how many slices did she need to cut each cake into?

   _____

4. Howie colored pictures of pinwheels. Each pinwheel had 5 sections. If Howie colored 13 sections, what was the least number of pinwheels in the coloring book? Write the sections colored as an improper fraction.

   _____

5. Kayla bought a bag of grapefruit. Each morning for 5 days she and her father each ate one half of a grapefruit. Her mother ate 3 halves total in that time. How much grapefruit did they eat altogether? Write your answer as an improper fraction and as a mixed number.

   _____

6. In the school walkathon, Bev walked $2\frac{1}{5}$ miles, Dennis walked $3\frac{2}{10}$ miles, and Natalie walked $2\frac{3}{5}$ miles. What was the total distance they walked? Write your answer as a whole number and as an improper fraction.

   _____

Use with text pp. 398–399

Compare and Order Fractions and Mixed Numbers

CA Standards
KEY NS 1.9, NS 1.5

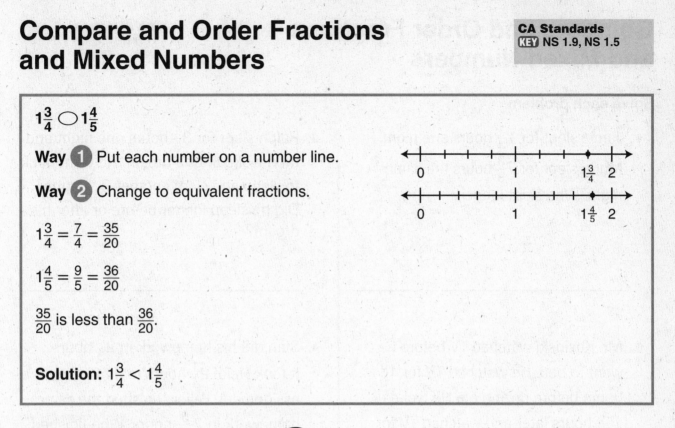

$1\frac{3}{4} \bigcirc 1\frac{4}{5}$

Way 1 Put each number on a number line.

Way 2 Change to equivalent fractions.

$1\frac{3}{4} = \frac{7}{4} = \frac{35}{20}$

$1\frac{4}{5} = \frac{9}{5} = \frac{36}{20}$

$\frac{35}{20}$ is less than $\frac{36}{20}$.

Solution: $1\frac{3}{4} < 1\frac{4}{5}$

Compare. Write >, <, or = for each $\bigcirc$.

1. $3\frac{2}{5} \bigcirc 3\frac{4}{10}$ _____

2. $2\frac{3}{7} \bigcirc 2\frac{1}{5}$ _____

3. $1\frac{3}{8} \bigcirc \frac{5}{4}$ _____

4. $\frac{1}{3} \bigcirc 1\frac{6}{9}$ _____

Spiral Review (Chapter 17, Lesson 2) **NS 1.5**

Find the fractional part of each number.

5. $\frac{1}{3}$ of 9 _____

6. $\frac{1}{2}$ of 10 _____

7. Colin has 36 bananas. One third of them are ripe. How many of the bananas are ripe? _____

Compare and Order Fractions and Mixed Numbers

Solve each problem.

1. Jamie slept for $7\frac{1}{4}$ hours one night. Maria slept for $7\frac{3}{8}$ hours the same night. Who slept longer?

2. Ralph slept for $3\frac{1}{3}$ hours one night and then woke after a dream. He went back to sleep and slept another $3\frac{3}{12}$ hours. Did he sleep longer before or after his dream?

3. Mr. Kosinski watched TV before he went to bed. He watched TV for $1\frac{3}{5}$ hours before dozing off. He woke up $1\frac{4}{10}$ hours later and watched TV for another $1\frac{4}{20}$ hours. Order these three periods of time from shortest to longest.

4. Stan did his homework in $2\frac{2}{3}$ hours. It took Heidi $2\frac{1}{4}$ hours to do the same assignment. Felicia finished the same homework in $2\frac{5}{12}$ hours. Who finished their homework in the shortest time? Who took the longest?

5. Steve jogged $2\frac{1}{2}$ miles on Monday, $2\frac{4}{5}$ miles on Wednesday, and $2\frac{6}{10}$ miles on Friday. Order his runs from shortest to longest using improper fractions.

6. Nancy lives $4\frac{2}{3}$ miles from her school. Dave lives $\frac{19}{4}$ miles from school. Raoul's house is $4\frac{2}{4}$ miles from school. Order the three distances from closest to farthest from school.

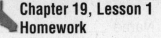
Hands On: Fractions and Decimals

Write the fraction that expresses the shaded part of the figure below.
Then write the decimal form of the fraction.

Step 1 Count the total number of parts that make up the grid. This grid contains 10 parts, and each part is 1 tenth. The total number of parts will be the denominator of the fraction.

Step 2 Now count the number of shaded parts. This grid has 4 shaded parts. The number of shaded parts will be the numerator of the fraction.

Step 3 Put together the numbers in the numerator and denominator to make the fraction: $\frac{4}{10}$.

Finally, write this fraction as a decimal: 0.4.

Solution: The shaded part of the figure is $\frac{4}{10}$ or 0.4.

Write the fraction that expresses the shaded parts of the figures
below. Then write the decimal form of each fraction.

1. _____   2. _____   3. _____   4. _____

Spiral Review (Chapter 11, Lesson 3) **KEY** NS 3.2, **KEY** NS 3.3

Multiply.

5. 28 × 20 _____   6. 74 × 40 _____

7. Ruth's family keeps compact disks in a wooden shelving unit. Each shelf holds 23 CDs, and the unit contains 12 shelves. How many CDs will fit in this shelving unit?

_____

Hands On: Fractions and Decimals

Write a fraction and a decimal to describe the shaded part of the model that represents each situation.

1. Georgette cut a pound cake into 10 pieces and served 4 of them to her friends.

_____

2. Howard colors twelve hundredths of a chart.

_____

3. Paige is in a choir with 9 other students. She says 5 other members are girls.

_____

4. Arthur's dad owns a small fruit stand. There are one hundred pieces of fruit on the stand. Forty-nine of them are oranges.

_____

5. Marcel, his two brothers, three cousins, and four aunts all went to the beach.

_____

6. Alicia's sister told her the best way to fall asleep is to count sheep. She decides she'll count up to 100. She starts, but loses count after 21. She tries again, but only makes it to 45 before falling asleep. What fraction of 100 sheep did she count before falling asleep?

_____

Mixed Numbers and Decimals

CA Standard
NS 1.0, NS 1.6

Write $4\frac{5}{10}$ as a decimal.

Step 1 Look at the number and decide which part is the whole number. In this mixed number, 4 is the whole number.

Step 2 Now say the fraction aloud in words. This part of the mixed number is five tenths. Identify the numerator (5) and the denominator (10).

Step 3 To write five tenths in decimal form, you will write the digit 5 from the numerator. The denominator tells you to place the 5 in the tenths place.

Solution: 4.5

Write each as a decimal.

1. $5\frac{9}{10}$

2. $7\frac{654}{1,000}$

3. $3\frac{86}{100}$

_____ _____ _____

Write the value of the digit 3 in each number.

4. 394.47

5. 24.03

6. 2,145.38

_____ _____ _____

Spiral Review (Chapter 19, Lesson 1) **NS 1.6**

Write each number as a fraction and as a decimal.

7. three tenths

8. one hundredth

_____ _____

9. Jan sliced a pie into 10 equal pieces. She and two friends ate 1 piece each. How much pie was left?

_____

Name _____ Date _____

Mixed Numbers and Decimals

CA Standards
NS 1.0, NS 1.6

Write each as a decimal.

1. How would you write $14\frac{23}{100}$ as a decimal?

_____

2. How would you write three and eight tenths as a decimal?

_____

3. How would you write $32\frac{75}{100}$ as a decimal?

_____

4. How would you write forty-two and seven tenths as a decimal?

_____

5. How would you write one hundred and two hundredths as a decimal?

_____

6. How would you write $851\frac{1}{100}$ as a decimal?

_____

Fractions and Decimal Equivalents

CA Standard
NS 1.6, NS 1.7

Write 0.4 as an equivalent fraction.

Step 1 Say the decimal aloud. This decimal is read four tenths. Write this number in fraction form.

$$\frac{4}{10}$$

Step 2 Think if there is smaller fraction that is equivalent. Both the numerator and the denominator can be divided by 2 to find an equivalent fraction of 2/5. It is also possible to express these fractions as hundredths. To find this fraction, both the numerator and the denominator can be multiplied by 10.

$$\frac{40}{100}$$

Solution: $0.4 = \frac{2}{5}$ or $\frac{4}{10}$ or $\frac{40}{100}$

Write each decimal as an equivalent fraction.

1. 0.74   **2.** 0.31   **3.** 0.25   **4.** 0.59

_____   _____   _____   _____

Write each fraction as an equivalent decimal.

5. $\frac{3}{5}$ **6.** $\frac{1}{4}$ **7.** $\frac{13}{20}$ **8.** $3\frac{1}{2}$

_____   _____   _____   _____

Spiral Review (Chapter 12, Lesson 2) **KEY** NS 3.2, **KEY** NS 3.0

Divide. Use multiplication to check.

9. $2\overline{)47}$ **10.** $3\overline{)52}$

11. Richard is placing 69 textbooks in a large classroom bookcase that has 4 shelves. All of the books will fit, but Richard wants the shelves to look equally full, if possible. How many books will Richard place on each of the 4 shelves?

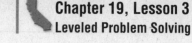
Fractions and Decimal Equivalents

Write a fraction to describe the shaded part of each model. Then write a decimal equivalent.

1. Hershel drew this picture to show the number of days out of the last 10 that he went to the library.

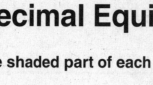

_____

2. Delia drew this model to show the number of days out of the last 10 that she practiced piano.

_____

3. Quentin has one hundred coins in a jar. Thirty-eight of them are pennies. The model shows the part of the coins that is pennies.

_____

4. Quentin also notices that 19 of the remaining coins are nickels. The model shows the part of the one hundred coins that isn't made up of pennies or nickels.

_____

5. Patricia bought a pack of 100 colorful hair beads. Her cousin Ellie weaves 51 beads into her hair. The model shows the part of the beads that Ellie does not weave into Patricia's hair.

_____

6. Patricia then weaves twenty-eight beads into Ellie's hair. Write a fraction and a decimal equivalent to describe the part of all the beads the girls weave into their hair.

_____

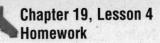
Compare and Order Decimals

CA Standard
KEY NS 1.2, NS 1.9

Compare 3.79 and 3.97. Write >, <, or = for the ◯.

3.79 ◯ 3.97

You can use a place-value chart.

ones		tenths	hundredths
3	.	7	9
3	.	9	7

Compare the numbers, starting from the left

Solution: 7 < 9, so **3.79 < 3.97**

Compare. Write >, <, or = for each ◯.

1. 23.23 ◯ 23.32

2. 7.8 ◯ 8.07

3. 6.600 ◯ 6.006

4. 12.40 ◯ 12.4

Order the numbers from least to greatest.

5. 38.42 3.842 0.384 3.084

6. 5.40 5.54 5.045 5.45

_____

_____

7. 7.59 7.05 57.01 7.95

8. 16.54 1.654 1.665 16.45

_____

_____

Spiral Review   (Chapter 15, Lesson 5) **KEY** NS 3.2, MR 3.2

Find the missing number.

9. 5 L = _____ mL

10. 2,000 g = _____ kg

11. Oriana has 6 bottles of spring water to take on a picnic.
Each bottle has a capacity of 500 mL. There are 1,000 milliliters
in 1 liter. How many liters of water can the 6 bottles hold?

_____

Compare and Order Decimals

Order each group of numbers as indicated.

1. How would you order the following decimals from least to greatest?

3.1   3.8   3.5   3.7

_____

2. How would you order the following decimals from greatest to least?

6.28   6.20   6.29   6.25

_____

3. How would you order the following decimals from least to greatest?

0.92   0.09   0.1   2.1

_____

4. How would you order the following decimals from greatest to least?

0.01   0.11   1.01   1.1

_____

5. How would you order the following decimals from least to greatest?

0.007   0.070   0.700   0.069

_____

6. How would you order the following decimals from greatest to least?

4.23   30.429   0.094   0.009

_____

Use with text pp. 426–427

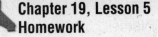

Compare and Order Fractions and Decimals

CA Standard
KEY NS 1.2, KEY NS 1.9

Compare $2\frac{1}{4}$ and 2.2. Write >, <, or = for the ◯.

$2\frac{1}{4}$ ◯ 2.2.

You can use a number line.

$2\frac{1}{4}$
2.2

2   3

Solution: $2\frac{1}{4}$ is to the right of 2.2, so $2\frac{1}{4} >$ 2.2.

Compare. Write >, <, or = for each ◯.

1. 5.2 ◯ $5\frac{2}{5}$

2. 37.42 ◯ $37\frac{42}{1,000}$

3. $6\frac{3}{4}$ ◯ 6.75

4. 8.054 ◯ $8\frac{54}{100}$

Order the numbers from greatest to least.

5. $3\frac{4}{5}$ 3.45   3.054 $3\frac{54}{100}$

6. 10.001   1.01 $10\frac{1}{100}$ $10\frac{1}{10}$

_____

7. 8.45   8.04 $8\frac{45}{1000}$ $8\frac{4}{1000}$

8. $1\frac{351}{1000}$ 1.03   1.65 $1\frac{39}{100}$

_____

Spiral Review   (Chapter 18, Lesson 2) **KEY** NS 1.9

Compare. Write >, <, or = for each ◯.

9. $\frac{2}{5}$ ◯ $\frac{4}{5}$

10. $\frac{2}{3}$ ◯ $\frac{4}{6}$

11. Two pizzas are the same size, but one has been sliced into 8 pieces and the second pizza has been sliced into 6 pieces. Derek ate 6 slices of the 8 from the first pizza. Carrie ate 5 slices of the 6 from the second pizza. Who ate more pizza? Express the amounts each person ate as fractions along with a >, <, or = symbol.

Compare and Order Fractions and Decimals

CA Standards
KEY NS 1.2, KEY NS 1.9

Order each group of numbers as indicated.

1. How would you order the following decimals and fractions from least to greatest?

$3\frac{2}{10}$ 3.02 $3\frac{8}{100}$ 3.009

_____

2. How would you order the following decimals and fractions from greatest to least?

4.16 $4\frac{8}{10}$ 4.9 $4\frac{21}{100}$

_____

3. How would you order the following decimals and fractions from least to greatest?

0.81 $\frac{8}{100}$ $\frac{3}{10}$ 1.3

_____

4. How would you order the following decimals and fractions from greatest to least?

$\frac{11}{100}$ 0.101   0.011 $\frac{111}{1,000}$

_____

5. How would you order the following decimals and fractions from least to greatest?

0.005 $\frac{50}{1,000}$ 0.500 $\frac{49}{100}$

_____

6. How would you order the following decimals and fractions from greatest to least?

$\frac{14}{10}$ 0.014 $\frac{14}{100}$ 1.1

_____

Name _____   Date _____

Hands On: Explore Addition and Subtraction of Decimals

CA Standards
NS 2.0, NS 2.1

Find the sum or difference. Use models if you wish.
1.73 + 0.68

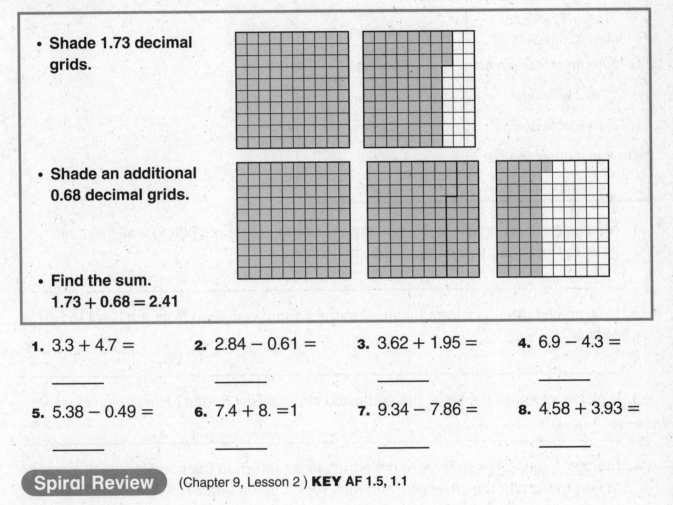

- Shade 1.73 decimal grids.

- Shade an additional 0.68 decimal grids.

- Find the sum.
  1.73 + 0.68 = 2.41

1. 3.3 + 4.7 =   **2.** 2.84 − 0.61 =   **3.** 3.62 + 1.95 =   **4.** 6.9 − 4.3 =

_____   _____   _____   _____

5. 5.38 − 0.49 =   **6.** 7.4 + 8. =1   **7.** 9.34 − 7.86 =   **8.** 4.58 + 3.93 =

_____   _____   _____   _____

Spiral Review   (Chapter 9, Lesson 2) **KEY** AF 1.5, 1.1

Find the rule.

9. Rule: _____

Input (a)	Output
12	6
20	10
28	14

10. Rule: _____

Input (b)	Output
12	21
34	43
57	66

11. The output values in a function table are 11, 17, and 23. The rule for the table is Output = 3m − 4. What are the input values?

_____

Explore Addition and Subtraction of Decimals

Solve each problem.

Distances from Hotel	
to San Francisco International Airport	14.5 miles
to Museum of Modern Art	3.6 miles
to Bay Bridge	2.8 miles
to Fort Mason	1.7 miles
to Aquarium of the Bay	0.5 miles
to Union Square	1.9 miles

1. Marcus can walk a mile in 15 minutes. How long will it take him to walk from his hotel to the aquarium and then back to his hotel?

   _____

2. How much farther is it from the hotel to the art museum than from the hotel to Fort Mason?

   _____

3. Which is closer to the hotel: the art museum or the Bay Bridge? How much closer?

   _____

4. Marcus' family plans to drive to the art museum, return to the hotel for lunch, drive to Fort Mason for the afternoon, and then return to the hotel. How far will they drive altogether?

   _____

5. Union Square is on the way to the airport from Marcus' hotel. His family plans to drive to Union Square, shop for 2 hours, and then drive to the airport. How long will their drive from Union Square to the airport be?

   _____

6. Marcus' sister can jog a mile in 7 minutes. Can she jog from the hotel to Fort Mason and back in less than half an hour? Explain your answer.

   _____

   _____

Name _____ Date _____

Round Decimals

Use rounding rules to round 9.75 to the nearest tenth.

Step 1 Find the place you want to round to.

9.7̲5

Step 2 Look at the digit to the right.

9.75

Step 3 Round as you do with whole numbers.

5 is greater than or equal to 5. So increase the tenths digit by one.

Solution: 9.75 rounds to 9.8.

Round each decimal to the nearest tenth.

1. 4.812 **2.** 7.234 **3.** 53.327 **4.** 20.481 **5.** 19.937

_____ _____ _____ _____ _____

Round each decimal to the place of the underlined digit.

6. 47̲.81 **7.** 8̲.8 **8.** 7.8̲1 **9.** 67̲.18 **10.** 51.9̲0

_____ _____ _____ _____ _____

11. 45̲.83 **12.** 958̲.66 **13.** 14.62̲1 **14.** 578.19̲6 **15.** 64.74̲9

_____ _____ _____ _____ _____

Spiral Review (Chapter 17, Lesson 5) **NS 1.5, NS 1.7**

Add or subtract.

16. $\frac{1}{6} + \frac{3}{6} =$ _____ **17.** $\frac{7}{15} + \frac{3}{15} =$ _____

18. Ted and Jackie shared a pizza. Ted ate $\frac{2}{8}$ of the pizza. Jackie ate $\frac{4}{8}$ of the pizza. How much of the pizza is left?

_____

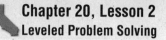
Round Decimals

Use the information from the signs to solve each problem.

Unleaded Regular	Unleaded Premium	Diesel
$1.89	**$1.94**	**$2.10**
a gallon	a gallon	a gallon

1. Tara's brother plans to pump 10 gallons of gas into the family car. He chooses unleaded regular gas. To the nearest dollar, about how much will the gas cost him?

_____

2. Tara's dad drives a sixteen-wheeler. It uses diesel as fuel. It has 2 fuel tanks. Each tank holds 75 gallons of diesel. Suppose both tanks are empty. If he buys enough diesel to fill both tanks, about how many dollars will the diesel cost?

_____

_____

3. Some vehicles are powered by gas. Others are powered by diesel. To the nearest tenth, how much less does the cheaper fuel cost?

_____

4. Micah's mother has 3 $10 bills. She wants to know about how many gallons of unleaded premium gas she can buy. Tell her a quick way to find the answer.

_____

_____

_____

5. Micah wants to know about how much less 26 gallons of unleaded regular costs than 26 gallons of unleaded premium. She has rounded the prices of the two grades of gasoline to the nearest tenth. Will this estimate give her the information she needs? Why or why not? _____

_____

6. Micah knows that their flower shop's delivery van uses 50 gallons of diesel a week. She estimates to the nearest dollar that they spend $600.00 on diesel each month. What has she done wrong? Write a mathematical sentence that will give her a better estimate.

_____

_____

Estimate Decimal Sums and Differences

CA Standards
NS 2.1, NS 2.2

Estimate by rounding to the nearest whole number.

```
7.5  →    8
+3.8 →  + 4    Add the
        ____   rounded
         12    numbers.
```
Solution: 7.5 + 3.8 is
about **12**.

1. 8.1
    − 6.6

2. $44.87
    + 58.16

3. $72.38
    − 60.08

4. 75.84
    −30.41

5. 22.987
    + 6.287

6. 546.8
    − 321.3

7. $309.55
    + 68.41

8. $365.27
    − 195.88

9. $917.35 + $342.32

10. $463.84 − $283.24

11. $583.37 + $418.94

12. $729.54 + $186.34

13. $741.65 − $387.14

14. $612.99 + $257.64

Spiral Review   (Chapter 9, Lesson 3) **KEY AF 1.5, AF 1.1**

Find the rule.

15. Rule: _____

Input (x)	Output (y)
21	14
35	28
49	42

16. Rule: _____

Input (m)	Output (n)
5	30
3	18
7	42

17. The output values in a function table are 7, 2, and 9. The rule for the table
is $x = y \div 9$. What are the (y) input values?

_____

Estimate Decimal Sums and Differences

CA Standards
NS 2.1, NS 2.2

Solve each problem.

1. How far does Jerry's mom drive to work each day? Write a mathematical sentence that shows the answer.

   _____

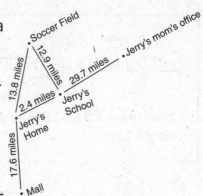

2. How much farther is it from Jerry's home to the mall than from Jerry's home to the soccer field? Write a mathematical sentence that shows the answer.

   _____

3. Jerry goes to the soccer field after school two days a week to practice. On Saturdays, he goes from his home to the soccer field to play a game. What is the difference in the length of his school day trip to school and to the soccer field and his Saturday trip to the field? Write a mathematical sentence that shows the answer.

   _____

4. Jerry's mom used to drive to her office 5 days a week. Now she works at home 2 days a week. How many fewer miles does she drive each week to and from her job? Write a mathematical sentence that shows the answer.

   _____

   _____

5. On Tuesday, Jerry's mom drove him to school and then went on to her office. After school, she picked him up and drove him home. That evening they went shopping at the mall. How many miles did Jerry's mom drive on Tuesday? Show your work.

   _____

   _____

6. Jerry's mom wants to watch his soccer practice. If she drives home first to change clothes, how much longer will her trip be than if she goes straight from the office to the practice? Write a mathematical sentence that shows the answer.

   _____

   _____

Add and Subtract Decimals

19.27 − 6.44	Write the decimal point	Estimate to check.
Line up the decimal points. Subtract.	in the answer.	Round and subtract.

19.27 − 6.44
Line up the decimal points.
Subtract.

$$\begin{array}{r} 19.27 \\ -6.44 \\ \hline \end{array}$$

Solution: 19.27 − 6.44 = 12.83

Write the decimal point in the answer.

$$\begin{array}{r} 19.27 \\ -6.44 \\ \hline 12.83 \end{array}$$

Estimate to check. Round and subtract.

$$\begin{array}{r} 19.27 \\ -6.44 \\ \hline \end{array} \begin{array}{r} \rightarrow \\ \rightarrow \end{array} \begin{array}{r} 19 \\ -6 \\ \hline \end{array}$$

12.83 is close to 13. The answer makes sense.

Add or subtract. Use estimation to check.

1. $\begin{array}{r} 6.08 \\ +4.80 \\ \hline \end{array}$
2. $\begin{array}{r} 7.9 \\ -3.4 \\ \hline \end{array}$
3. $\begin{array}{r} \$22.49 \\ +18.74 \\ \hline \end{array}$
4. $\begin{array}{r} \$39.45 \\ -28.74 \\ \hline \end{array}$
5. $\begin{array}{r} 7.09 \\ +6.81 \\ \hline \end{array}$

6. $\begin{array}{r} 3.95 \\ +7.55 \\ \hline \end{array}$
7. $\begin{array}{r} 15.21 \\ -8.54 \\ \hline \end{array}$
8. $\begin{array}{r} 65.87 \\ +22.95 \\ \hline \end{array}$
9. $\begin{array}{r} \$14.87 \\ -5.23 \\ \hline \end{array}$
10. $\begin{array}{r} \$23.16 \\ +15.46 \\ \hline \end{array}$

Place the decimal points in the addends to make the sentences correct.

11. $207 + 35 + 629 = 11.86$ _____

12. $427 + 138 + 29 = 59.4$ _____

13. $115 + 283 + 026 = 14.59$ _____

Spiral Review (Chapter 9, Lesson 3) **KEY** AF 1.1, MR 1.5

Complete the table.

14. **Rule:** $y = 4x - 5$

Input (x)	Output (y)
3	
5	
7	

15. **Rule:** $a = 7(b \times 2)$

Input (a)	Output (b)
42	
98	
28	

Add and Subtract Decimals

CA Standards
NS 2.1, NS 2.2

The Bay Area Rapid Transit provides mass transportation for the San Francisco Bay area. In 2003, the system opened a station at the San Francisco International Airport (SFO). Many people are now taking a BART train from a station near their homes or hotels to the airport instead of driving or taking a taxi.

Use the information from the map and table to solve the problems.

BART Rates To and From	
San Francisco International Airport (SFO)	
from the Embarcadero Hotel	$5.15
from Daly City	$4.50
from Oakland Airport	$5.80
from San Leandro	$6.05
from Richmond	$6.15

1. What does a round trip on BART from San Leandro to the San Francisco International Airport cost? _____

2. Which costs more: the trip to the airport from the Embarcadero or the trip from Richmond? How much more? _____

3. A taxi ride from SFO to the Embarcadero in San Francisco costs about $31.00. Would it cost less for Janet, her two sisters, her mom, and her dad to hire a taxi to take them to the Embarcadero or to take BART? Explain your answer.

_____

4. Grace and Jennifer are planning to take a trip to Los Angeles together. Grace and her mom will ride BART from San Leandro to SFO. They will meet Jennifer along the way at the BART station in Daly City. When they return from Los Angeles, all three will take BART back to their homes. They have budgeted $30.00 for BART tickets. Will $30.00 be enough? Explain your answer.

_____

5. Wayne and his family live in Richmond. Wayne and his mom are planning to ride BART to SFO to meet his grandmother. Then they will all three ride BART back to Richmond. How much will they spend in all? _____

6. The price of BART tickets is based on the distance traveled. How much would a ticket from the Oakland Airport to Daly City cost? Explain your answer.

_____

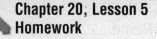
Problem Solving: Work Backward

CA Standards
2.6, NS 2.0

Use a work backward strategy to solve each problem.

Barry bought 8 fancy guppies and 3 goldfish for his aquarium. He spent $16.49. If each goldfish cost 99¢, how much does each fancy guppy cost?

Step 1 Find the cost of the goldfish.

$3 \times 99¢ = \$2.97$

Step 2 Find the cost of the fancy guppies.

$\$16.49 - 2.97 = \$13.52$

Step 3 Find the cost of each fancy guppy.

$\$13.52 \div 8 = \$1.69$

Solution: Each fancy guppy costs $1.69.

---

1. Casey can put 8 cards on a page in an album. He puts 400 cards into the album. How many pages does he use?

   _____

2. Franco buys 5 cans of tomato soup and 4 cans of noodle soup. He spends $6.61. If the tomato soup costs 69¢ per can, how much do all the cans of noodle soup cost?

   _____

3. Heather and two of her classmates, Lindsey and Wanda, go to a ballet recital with Heather's mother. They paid $31.50. If an adult ticket cost $12.60, how much does one student ticket cost?

   _____

Spiral Review (Chapter 19, Lesson 2) **NS 1.0, NS 1.6**

4. Write the value of the digit 9 in 31.9̲87. _____

5. Write thirty-six and thirty-six hundredths as a decimal. _____

6. Sam has $7\frac{17}{20}$ dollars. Write $7\frac{17}{20}$ as a decimal. _____

Problem Solving: Work Backward

Solve each problem by working backwards.

1. Colleen bought 6 yards of material and a bag of buttons. She spent a total of $28. The buttons cost $2.50. How much was each yard of material?

_____

2. Paul cut a pole into 5 equal parts. He then cut 3.7 inches off the last piece. The length of the part left was 2.3 inches. How long was the original pole?

_____

3. Mr. Quibley takes his fourth-grade class to the planetarium. The cost for him and his students is $93.75. If the cost of an adult ticket is $7.50 and the cost of a student ticket is $3.75, how many students are in Mr. Quibley's class?

_____

4. Shaun bought 6 pizzas and 3 salads for $95.49. Each salad cost $5.85. What is the cost of each pizza?

_____

5. A steak dinner with an appetizer and a dessert costs $19.95 at a local restaurant. If the appetizer costs twice as much as the desert and the desert costs $2.50, how much does the steak cost?

_____

6. Nadia has $17.67 in her piggy bank. That is $1.17 more than twice the amount of money in her brother Ivan's piggy bank. How much does Ivan have in his bank?

_____

Hands On: Plot Points

CA Standards
KEY MG 2.0, MR 2.3

Use the graph on the right for Exercises 1–8. Write the letter of the point for each ordered pair.

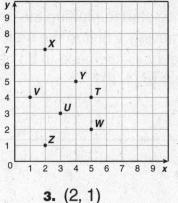

> **What is the letter for (5, 4).**
>
> Start at 0.
>
> Move right 5 units.
>
> Then move up 4 units.
>
> **Solution:** Point T is at (5, 4).

1. (1, 4)   **2.** (2, 7)   **3.** (2, 1)

_____   _____   _____

Write the ordered pair for each point

4. U   **5.** W   **6.** Y

_____   _____   _____

7. Which coordinates of point X and point Z are the same?
Which are different?

_____

8. Write directions explaining how to plot (2, 7).

_____

Spiral Review (Chapter 19, Lesson 4) **KEY NS 1.2**

Use symbols <, > or = to complete the number sentence.

9. 6.53 $\bigcirc$ 6.55

10. 0.95 $\bigcirc$ 0.09

11. Benji's backpack weighs 10.9 pounds and Rajani's backpack
weighs 10.88 pounds. Which backpack is heavier?

_____

Homework

187

Use with text pp. 466–467

Hands On: Plot Points

CA Standards
KEY MG 2.0, MR 2.3

Solve.

1. Aimee started plotting the point (1, 2) by moving 1 unit to the right of (0, 0). What does she need to do next in order to get to (1, 2)?

_____

2. Ahn-Lee plotted the points (3, 3) and (3, 7). If she connects the points, what type of line will she form, vertical, horizontal or neither? Explain.

_____

_____

_____

_____

3. Nick plotted the point (2, 4) and wants to plot another point to draw a horizontal line. Write one possible ordered pair for the other point he can plot.

_____

_____

4. Marlon plotted the point (1, 5) and wants to plot another point to draw a vertical line. Write one possible ordered pair for the other point he can plot.

_____

_____

5. Davita plotted the point (5, 8) by moving to the right 8 units and up 5 units. What did she do wrong?

_____

_____

_____

6. Ben found one point on a horizontal line to be (4, 7). What are the coordinates of another point on the line?

_____

_____

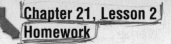
Plot and Name Points on a Grid

CA Standard
KEY MG 2.0

Plot each point and label it with the correct letter on the grid.

Example *Z* (3, 5)

- Start at 0.
- Move right 3 units.
- Then move up 5 units.
- Then make a dot on the point.
- Label the point *Z*.

Solution:

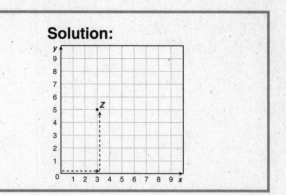

1. *A* (1, 3)　　　　2. *B* (3, 2)

3. *C* (4, 4)　　　　4. *D* (2, 5)

5. *E* (0, 6)　　　　6. *F* (6, 3)

7. *G* (5, 0)　　　　8. *H* (2, 1)

9. *I* (4, 1)　　　　10. *J* (2, 2)

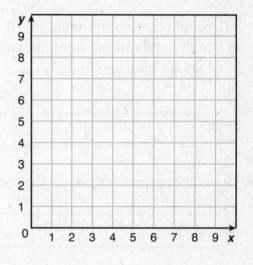

Spiral Review (Chapter 14, Lesson 2) **NS 4.0, NS 4.1**

Use divisibility rules to tell if 2, 3, 5, or 9 are factors of the given numbers.

11. 55

_____

12. 492

_____

13. A full basket contains 6 oranges. If Teo has 78 oranges, will he have any left over after filling all of his baskets?

_____

Plot and Name Points on a Grid

CA Standards
KEY MG 2.0, MR 2.3

Solve.

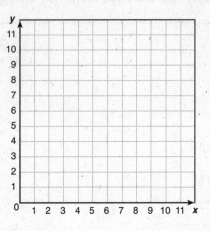

1. Kaitlin plotted the point (1, 8). How many units to the right did she move? Explain how you know.

_____
_____
_____
_____

2. Max plotted the point (4, 9). How many units up did he move? Explain how you know.

_____
_____
_____
_____

3. What can you say if two points have the same first coordinate?

_____
_____

4. Write instructions to plot the point (3, 9).

_____
_____

5. If David plotted (2, 5) and (4, 5), can he connect the two points with a vertical line? Why or why not?

_____
_____
_____

6. On the graph of a square, one corner is (1, 2) and another is (2, 3). What are the other two corners of the square?

_____
_____
_____

Use with text pp. 468–471

Graphs of Functions

CA Standards
KEY MG 2.0, **KEY** MG 2.1

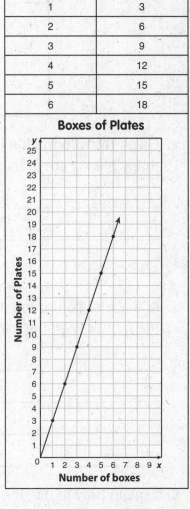

Boxes of Plates
$y = 3x$

Number of boxes (x)	Number of plates (y)
1	3
2	6
3	9
4	12
5	15
6	18

Boxes of Plates

Example:

Sarah is packing plates into boxes. Each box can fit 3 plates. She wants to know how many plates are in 6 boxes.

Find the number of plates by graphing the function $y = 3x$.

Step 1 **Plot** and **connect** the points from the table. Use the number of boxes as the x-coordinate and the number of plates as the y-coordinate.

Step 2 **Extend** the line segment to see how many plates will fit into larger numbers of boxes. The points should lie on a line.

Step 3 Find the point on the line for 6 boxes. Start at 0 and move 6 units to the right to match the number of boxes. Then move up to the meet the line at (6, 18).

Solution: There are 18 plates in 6 boxes.

1. Extend the graph. Find the number of plates in 8 boxes.

_____

2. Thirty-six plates are in boxes. How many boxes were used.

_____

Spiral Review (Chapter 16, Lesson 2) **KEY** NS 1.8, NS 1.0

Use the symbols <, > or = to complete the number sentence.

3. ⁻3 ◯ 5

4. ⁻8 ◯ ⁻10

5. Which is greater, the difference between ⁻8 and ⁺4 or the difference between ⁻1 and ⁺12?

_____

Graphs of Functions

CA Standards
KEY MG 2.0, MR 2.1

Use the table below to solve the following problems.

Number of Packages of Gum	Total Number of Pieces of Gum
1	4
2	8
3	12
4	16
5	20

1. Given the information in the table, how many pieces are in each pack of gum?

_____

_____

2. Plot the points in the table on a separate piece of graph paper.

_____

_____

_____

3. In the function graph above, what is the input? What is the output?

_____

_____

_____

4. Extend your graph and tell the number of pieces in 8 packs of gum.

_____

_____

_____

5. Explain how to use the same function graph to determine the number of wheels on a certain number of cars.

_____

_____

_____

_____

_____

6. What if each pack of gum contained 8 pieces. How would your table and function graph be different?

_____

_____

Graph Equations

CA Standards
KEY MG 2.0, KEY MG 2.1

Example:

Draw a graph to represent the equation $y = 2x + 2$

**Step ① ** Use the equation to make a function table. Choose numbers to make the values of y easy to find.

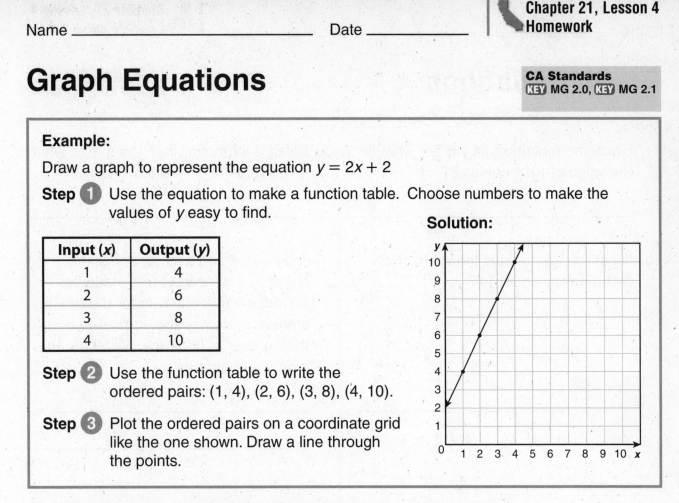

Solution:

Input (x)	Output (y)
1	4
2	6
3	8
4	10

**Step ② ** Use the function table to write the ordered pairs: (1, 4), (2, 6), (3, 8), (4, 10).

**Step ③ ** Plot the ordered pairs on a coordinate grid like the one shown. Draw a line through the points.

For each equation, complete the function table. Then on a separate piece of graph paper, graph the equation.

1. $y = x - 2$

Input (x)	Output (y)

2. $y = 3x + 1$

Input (x)	Output (y)

3. $y = 10$

Input (x)	Output (y)

Spiral Review (Chapter 20, Lesson 2) **NS 2.2, MR 2.5**

Solve.

4. Round 4.56 to the nearest tenth.

_____

5. Round 2.302 to the nearest whole number.

_____

6. If you buy three sandwiches for $6.75 each, will the total be closer to $18 or $21?

_____

Graph Equations

CA Standards
KEY MG 2.0, **KEY** MG 2.1

Solve.

1. Given the function rule $y = 2x$, what is the value of y if x equals 2?

   _____

2. Given the function rule $y = x + 3$, what is the value of y if x equals 4?

   _____

3. If $y = 3x + 2$, what is the value of x that makes y equal 11?

   _____

4. Julie is opening a lemonade stand. If she sells each cup of lemonade for $2, write a function rule for the total amount of money she earns based on the number of cups sold. What are the inputs and outputs?

   _____

   _____

   _____

   _____

   _____

5. Matteo and Mohammed are competing in a bike race. Matteo bikes 15 miles in one hour and Mohammed bikes 18 miles in one hour. Use a function rule to determine how far Matteo and Mohammed have biked after two hours. What is the difference between their distances?

   _____

   _____

   _____

   _____

6. In the example in problem 5, suppose that after 2 hours, Matteo kept biking for an additional hour, and Mohammed stopped to eat lunch. After 3 hours, how far ahead of Mohammed will Matteo be?

   _____

   _____

   _____

   _____

Name _____ Date _____

Problem Solving: Use a Graph

CA Standards
KEY MG 2.1, MR 2.3

The local movie theater is having a deal for matinee movies. The first person in a group pays full price, and each other person in the group gets a discount. The graph shows the relationship between the number of people in a group and the cost of their tickets. Use the graph to solve each problem.

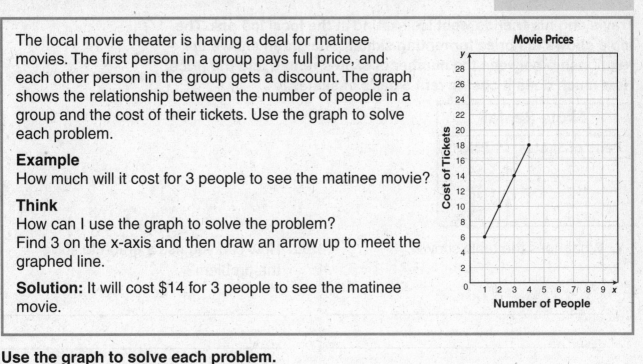

Movie Prices

Example
How much will it cost for 3 people to see the matinee movie?

Think
How can I use the graph to solve the problem?
Find 3 on the x-axis and then draw an arrow up to meet the graphed line.

Solution: It will cost $14 for 3 people to see the matinee movie.

Use the graph to solve each problem.

1. How much more would it cost for 6 people to see the matinee movie than for 4 people to see the matinee movie?

   _____

2. A group of people spent a total of $22 on tickets and snacks for the matinee movie. If the group spent $8 on snacks, how many people were in the group?

   _____

3. John has $30 to spend on matinee tickets. What is the greatest number of people including himself that he can buy tickets for? How much money will he have left?

   _____

Spiral Review (Chapter 19, Lesson 4) **KEY NS 1.2**

Fill in the box with <, > or =.

4. 0.54 ☐ 0.094

5. 7.6 ☐ 0.76

6. Mandy has 0.4 pounds of ice cream. Luis has 0.9 pounds of ice cream. Who has more ice cream?

_____

Problem Solving: Use a Graph

CA Standards
KEY MG 2.1, MR 2.3

Travis and his friends went ice skating at the local ice rink. The table shows the price for renting skates. The graph shows the relationship between the number of skates rented and the price. How much does it cost to rent 5 pairs of skates?

Skate Rental

Pairs of Skates	Price
1	$4
2	$8
3	$12

1. What does the table show?

_____

_____

2. How can you use a graph to solve the problem?

_____

_____

3. Plot the graph of the data in the table on the grid below.

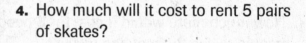

_____

_____

4. How much will it cost to rent 5 pairs of skates?

_____

5. How does the graph relate to the table?

_____

_____

6. What if the price for skates were $6 for 1 pair, $10 for two pairs and $14 for three pairs. How would this affect your graph above?

_____

_____

Hands On: Graph Ordered Pairs of Integers

CA Standards
KEY MG 2.0, **KEY** NS 1.8

Find (2, −3) on the coordinate plane.

Step 1 Start at the origin. 2 is the x-coordinate and it is positive. So move right 2 units.

Step 2 −3 is the y-coordinate and it is negative. So move down 3 units.

Find the point on the coordinate plane.

1. (3, 4). Label it *A*.

2. (⁻2, 6). Label it *B*.

3. (5, ⁻5). Label it *C*.

4. (⁻4, ⁻2). Label it *D*.

Write the coordinates of the point.

5. *E* _____

6. *F* _____

7. *G* _____

8. *H* _____

Spiral Review   (Chapter 21, Lesson 3) **KEY** MG 2.1, **KEY** MG 2.0

9. Plot point (1, 3) on the coordinate grid.

10. Plot point (2, 6) on the coordinate grid.

11. Points (1, 3) and (2, 6) are on the graph of the equation $y = 3x$. What are two other points on that graph?

_____

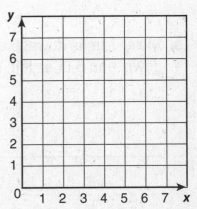

Use with text pp. 486–487

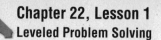
Hands On: Graph Ordered Pairs of Integers

CA Standards
KEY MG 2.0, KEY NS 1.8

Find the locations on a coordinate plane. For Problems 2–6, you begin with the answer of the problem before.

1. Begin at the origin (0, 0). Move 6 units right and 4 units up. Where are you?

   _____

2. Move 5 units up and 6 units left. Where are you?

   _____

3. Move 3 units left, 5 units down, and 2 units left. Where are you?

   _____

4. Move 8 units down, 7 units right, and 4 units up. Where are you?

   _____

5. Move 7 units down, 5 units left, 5 units down, and 5 units left. Where are you?

   _____

6. Move 3 units up, 2 units right, 3 units up, 2 units right, 3 units up, 2 units right, 3 units up, and 2 units right. Where are you?

   _____

Graph Ordered Pairs of Integers

CA Standards
KEY MG 2.0, KEY NS 1.8

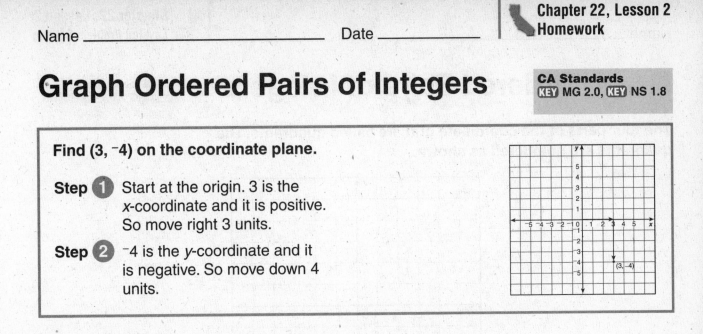

Find (3, ⁻4) on the coordinate plane.

Step 1 Start at the origin. 3 is the *x*-coordinate and it is positive. So move right 3 units.

Step 2 ⁻4 is the *y*-coordinate and it is negative. So move down 4 units.

Find, mark, and label the following points on the coordinate plane.

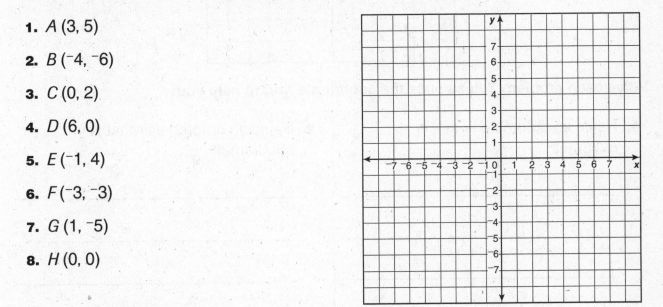

1. *A* (3, 5)

2. *B* (⁻4, ⁻6)

3. *C* (0, 2)

4. *D* (6, 0)

5. *E* (⁻1, 4)

6. *F* (⁻3, ⁻3)

7. *G* (1, ⁻5)

8. *H* (0, 0)

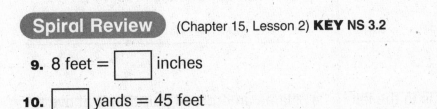

Spiral Review (Chapter 15, Lesson 2) **KEY NS 3.2**

9. 8 feet = ☐ inches

10. ☐ yards = 45 feet

11. It is 3 miles from Sally's home to school. How many feet is that?

_____

Name _____ Date _____

Graph Ordered Pairs of Integers

CA Standards
KEY MG 2.0, **KEY** NS 1.8

The four parts of the coordinate grid are called quadrants. The quadrants are numbered as shown.

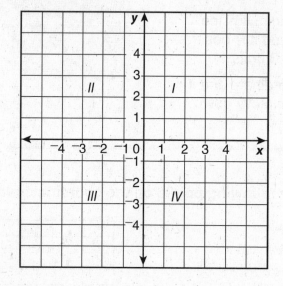

Solve each problem. You can use the coordinate grid to help you.

1. Name an ordered pair that is in quadrant I.

_____

_____

_____

2. Name an ordered pair that is in quadrant III.

_____

_____

_____

3. In which quadrant is (25, ⁻18)?

_____

4. In which quadrant is (⁻43, 77)?

_____

5. Name an ordered pair that is to the left of the *y*-axis and isn't in any quadrant.

_____

_____

6. Name an ordered pair that is above the *x*-axis and isn't in any quadrant.

_____

_____

Leveled Problem Solving
200
Use with text pp. 488–491

Lengths of Horizontal and Vertical Line Segments

CA Standards
KEY MG 2.2, KEY MG 2.3

- To find the length of a **horizontal** line segment, find the difference between the *x*-coordinates:

  distance from (**2**, 3) to (**6**, 3) = 6 − 2 = 4 units

- To find the length of a vertical line segment, find the difference between the *y*-coordinates:

  distance from (8, **7**) to (8, **2**) = 7 − 2 = 5 units

Graph each pair of points. Find the length of the segment that connects each pair of points.

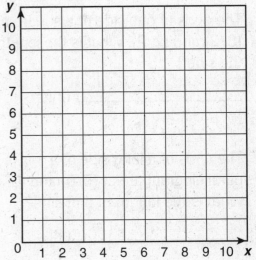

1. (6, 3) (6, 9) _____

2. (1, 2) (5, 2) _____

3. (5, 10) (10, 10) _____

4. (0, 0) (0, 8) _____

5. (2, 6) (2, 10) _____

6. (3, 0) (9, 0) _____

Spiral Review (Chapter 21, Lesson 2) **KEY MG 2.0, MR 2.3**

Plot each point and label it.

7. *A* (4, 5)

8. *B* (0, 3)

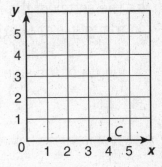

9. What are the coordinates of point *C* on the coordinate grid?

_____

Lengths of Horizontal and Vertical Line Segments

CA Standards
KEY MG 2.2, **KEY** MG 2.3

Solve each problem. You can use the coordinate grid to help you.

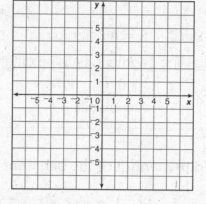

1. The ends of one side of a square are at (3, 2) and (7, 2). What is the length of the side?

   _____ units

2. The ends of a side of a rectangle are at (4, 1) and (4, 10). What is the length of that side?

   _____ units

3. The ends of a long side of a parallelogram are at (0, 0) and (0, 44). What is the length of that side?

   _____ units

4. The ends of one base of a trapezoid are at (25, 75) and (150, 75). What is the length of that side?

   _____ units

5. The vertex of the right angle of a right triangle is at (1, 1). The other vertices are at (5, 1) and (1, 4). What is the length of the side parallel to the x-axis?

   _____ units

6. An isosceles triangle has vertices at (2, 0), (6, 0), and (4, 8). What is the length of the altitude?

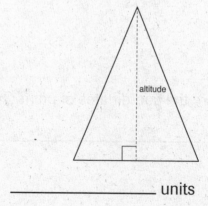

   _____ units

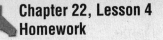
Line Segments in the Coordinate Grid

CA Standards
KEY MG 2.2, **KEY** MG 2.3

How long is line segment *AB*?

To find the length of a line segment, you can count the units, or you can find the difference between the coordinates.

- Count the units: 2, 3, 4, 5 = 3 units
- Subtract the *x*-coordinates: 5 − 2 = 3 units

Solution: Line segment AB is 3 units long.

Graph and connect each pair of points. Then count units to find the length of the line segment.

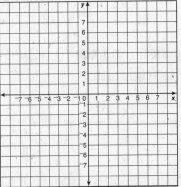

1. (1, ⁻2) (7, ⁻2) _____

2. (⁻6, ⁻5) (5, ⁻5) _____

3. (0, ⁻1) (0, 6) _____

Subtract to find the length of the line segment that connects each pair of points.

4. (⁻3, 6) (⁻3, 10) _____   5. (⁻8, 2) (⁻3, 2) _____

Spiral Review   (Chapter 18, Lessons 2–4) **KEY** NS 1.9

6. Compare. Write >, <, or = for the ⬭. $\frac{3}{4}$ ⬭ $\frac{1}{2}$

7. One worm is $1\frac{1}{2}$ inches long. Another worm is $1\frac{3}{8}$ inches long.

   Which worm is longer? _____ inches.

Line Segments in the Coordinate Grid

CA Standards
KEY MG 2.2, **KEY** MG 2.3

Use subtraction or counting to find the distance between the points. You can use the coordinate grid to help you.

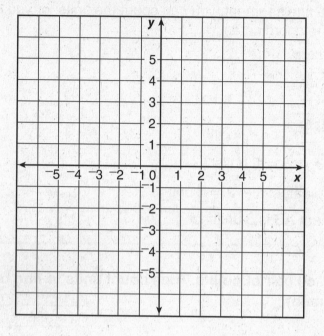

1. A raccoon ran from (0, 12) to (0, ⁻8). How far did it run?

   _____ units

2. A swan swam from (10, 6) to (⁻3, 6). How far did it swim?

   _____ units

3. A giraffe galloped from (⁻3, 4) to (⁻3, ⁻9) and back to (⁻3, 4). How far did it gallop?

   _____ units

4. A lion leaped from (7, 0) to (⁻4, 0). Then it leaped to (0, 0). How far did it leap?

   _____ units

5. A walrus walked from (6, ⁻8) to (6, 6) to (⁻3, 6). How far did it walk?

   _____ units

6. A hare hopped from (⁻2, 3) to (⁻2, ⁻5). It stopped to eat some carrots. Then it hopped to (7, ⁻5). It took a nap. It hopped home to (7, 0). How far did it hop?

   _____ units

Hands On: Collect and Organize Data

CA Standards
SDAP 1.1, SDAP 1.0

Complete the tally chart. Then use it for problems 1–5.

Favorite Color		
Color	**Tally**	**Number**
Yellow	卌 |||	
Blue	卌	
Red	卌 ||	
Green	||||	

How many students choose red?

Step **1** Count the tallies for red.
Remember that 卌 stands for 5.

Step **2** Add 5 + 2.

Solution: Seven students choose red.

1. Which answer was given the most often? the least often?
   _____

2. How many classmates answered the survey question?
   _____

3. What is the order of colors from least popular to most popular?
   _____

4. Did half of the people surveyed choose either red or blue? Explain.
   _____

5. Did more people choose yellow than green and blue combined? Explain.
   _____
   _____

Spiral Review (Chapter 19, Lesson 1) **NS 1.6**

Add or subtract each set of numbers and round the answer to the nearest whole number.

6. 4.82 + 6.45 = _____

7. 3.61 − 1.24 = _____

8. Ron drove 4.21 miles to his friend's house. Then he drove 3.17 miles to the movies. About how many miles did Ron drive in all?
   _____

Hands On: Collect and Organize Data

CA Standards
SDAP 1.1, SDAP 1.0

Amelia surveyed the students in her class on their favorite kind of television program. The results are given in the tally chart below. Use the information in the chart to solve the problems.

Favorite Kind of Television Program		
Program	Tally	Number
sitcom	卌 |||	8
reality shows	卌		6
news	|||	3
sports	卌	5
talk show	||||	4

1. What program is most popular with students? Which is least popular?

_____

2. Which program ranks third in this survey?

_____

3. What is the total number of people surveyed?

_____

4. Which two programs combined account for 14 votes?

_____

_____

5. Which two programs combined are one more than the number of people who like reality shows?

_____

6. Which three programs combined equal half of the total votes?

_____

_____

Use with text pp. 512–513

Name _____ Date _____

Chapter 23, Lesson 2
Homework

Median and Mode

CA Standard
SDAP 1.1, SDAP 1.2

Order the data from least to greatest. Find the median, mode, and outlier of each set of data.

↓ 13, 36, 42, 51, 51, 62, 67 The middle value is 51. **The median of the data is 51.**	↓ ↓ 13, 36, 42, 51, 51, 62, 67 The number most distant from the other data is 13. **The outlier of the data is 13.**

1. 34, 49, 37, 29, 34

2. 9, 21, 93, 31, 31

_____

_____

_____

3. 24, 20, 24, 12, 60

4. 74, 110, 67, 45, 67

_____

_____

_____

Spiral Review (Chapter 19, Lesson 5) **KEY** NS 1.2, **KEY** NS 1.9

Order the numbers from least to greatest.

5. 3.32, 3.36, $2\frac{1}{2}$, 3.21, $2\frac{2}{5}$

6. $7\frac{1}{4}$, 7.98, 7.66, 7.91, $7\frac{1}{3}$

_____

7. Lucy, Fred, and Juan were in a broad jump contest. Lucy jumped 3.5 feet, Fred jumped $4\frac{1}{4}$ feet, and Juan jumped $3\frac{4}{10}$ feet. Write their names in order of their jumps from greatest to least.

_____

Homework
Copyright © Houghton Mifflin Company. All rights reserved.

207

Use with text pp. 514–517

Median and Mode

CA Standards
SDAP 1.1, SDAP 1.2

Mrs. Iko asked for 7 volunteers to help teach median, mode, and outlier. The volunteers measured their heights in centimeters. The table at the right shows the results.

Mrs. Iko's Class	
Name	Height (cm)
Bell	116
Dale	124
Lucy	121
Mike	128
Gina	124
Georgia	119
Jay	122

1. Arrange the data in the table from least to greatest.

   _____

   _____

2. What are the median, the mode, and the outlier, if any?

   _____

   _____

3. Mrs. Iko added her own height to the table. She is 170 centimeters tall. How will this information change the median?

   _____

   _____

4. What changes are there to the mode and the outlier?

   _____

   _____

   _____

5. Mrs. Iko removed her height and Dale's height from the table. How did this change the median?

   _____

   _____

6. What, if any, changes did it make to the mode and the outlier? Explain.

   _____

   _____

   _____

   _____

Name _____ Date _____

Hands On: Double Bar Graphs

CA Standards
SDAP 1.3, SDAP 1.0

During which month did San Francisco
have more rainy days than Portland?

Step **1** Compare the bar for San Francisco and
the bar for Portland during each month.

Step **2** In July, there were 10 rainy days in Portland
and 11 rainy days in San Francisco.

Solution: During the month of July, San Francisco
had more rainy days than Portland.

Jessie made a table to show the scores for his team and the
opposing team in the first three games of the season. Use the
table to make a double bar graph. Use the graph to answer each
question.

Points Scored in Each Game			
Team	Game 1	Game 2	Game 3
Goldenrods	47	51	63
Opponents	42	55	57

1. What interval did you choose for your graph? Explain your choice.

_____

2. During which game did the opponents score more points than the

Goldenrods? _____

Spiral Review (Chapter 19, Lesson 1) NS 1.6

Add or subtract and round the answer to the nearest whole number.

3. $8.22 - 3.40 =$ _____   **4.** $4.52 + 5.61 =$ _____

5. Nancy has 5.37 feet of material. She uses 2.74 feet to make a
curtain. About how many feet of material does she have left?

_____

Hands On: Double Bar Graphs

CA Standards
SDAP 1.3, SDAP 1.0

The outdoor arena in Hillary's town is used regularly for both sporting events and musical concerts. The double bar graph below shows the attendance for each kind of event for a 3-month period. Use the data to solve the problems.

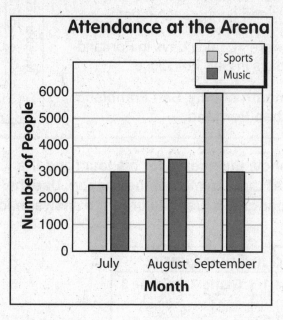

1. In what month did music attendance at the arena outnumber sporting events attendance?

   _____

2. In what month was attendance for both kinds of events equal?

   _____

3. In which month did sports attendance double that of music concert attendance?

   _____

4. By how much did attendance of sporting events grow from July to August?

   _____

5. What was the total attendance of all sporting events from July to September?

   _____

6. How many more people would have had to attend concerts to equal the attendance of sporting events during this 3-month period?

   _____

Name _____ Date _____

Read and Understand Line Graphs

CA Standards
SDAP 1.0, SDAP 1.3

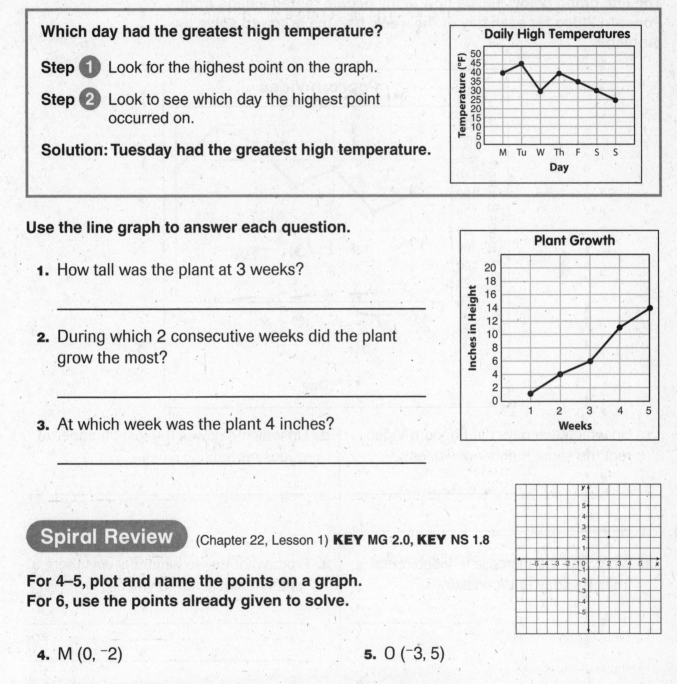

Which day had the greatest high temperature?

Step 1 Look for the highest point on the graph.

Step 2 Look to see which day the highest point occurred on.

Solution: Tuesday had the greatest high temperature.

Daily High Temperatures

Use the line graph to answer each question.

1. How tall was the plant at 3 weeks?

_____

2. During which 2 consecutive weeks did the plant grow the most?

_____

3. At which week was the plant 4 inches?

_____

Plant Growth

Spiral Review (Chapter 22, Lesson 1) **KEY** MG 2.0, **KEY** NS 1.8

For 4–5, plot and name the points on a graph.
For 6, use the points already given to solve.

4. M (0, ‾2)   **5.** O (‾3, 5)

6. Mike wanted to plot 3 points to represent the corners of a triangle. He plotted the 2 points shown. What should the coordinates of the third point be?

_____

Read and Understand Line Graphs

CA Standards
SDAP 1.0, SDAP 1.3

The line graph below shows how many people rented videos from Popcorn Video for each day of the week. Use the graph to solve the problems.

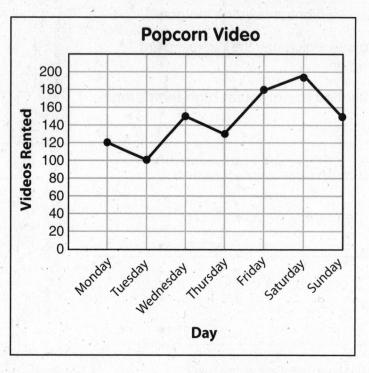

1. On which two days did Popcorn Video rent the same number of videos?

_____

_____

2. On which day was the least number of videos rented?

_____

_____

3. What was the increase in video rental from Tuesday to Wednesday?

_____

4. From what day to what day was there a rental decrease of 45 videos?

_____

5. How many more videos did Popcorn Video rent on its busiest day than on its slowest day?

_____

6. What was the total number of videos rented from Friday through Sunday at Popcorn Video?

_____

Problem Solving: Show Data in Different Ways

The graph shows student scores on a test based on the number of hours of sleep the night before. What score should a student expect if he/she got 8 hours of sleep?

Look at the data points that are above 8 hours of sleep. They are both above 90.

Test Scores Based on Hours of Sleep

Solution: A student could expect a score of 90 or greater.

Use the scatter plot to solve the following problems.

1. Would it be reasonable to represent this data in a double bar graph? Explain why or why not?

_____

_____

_____

2. Why do you think some students that got more sleep got a lower test score than some students that got less sleep?

_____

_____

Spiral Review (Chapter 22, Lesson 4) **KEY** MG 2.2, **KEY** MG 2.3

Graph each pair of points on a separate sheet of paper. Find the length of the line segment that connects each pair of points.

3. (1,3) and (1,10) _____

4. (2,4) and (5,4) _____

5. The length of the segment connecting point A and point B is 4. If the coordinates of point A are (2,7) and the coordinates of point B are (2, ☐), what are possible values for the ☐ ? _____

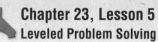

Problem Solving: Show Data in Different Ways

CA Standards
MR 2.3, SDAP 1.0

Use the double bar graph to solve Problems 1–3. Use the scatter plot to solve Problems 4–6. The scatter plot shows the height of various children in inches based on age.

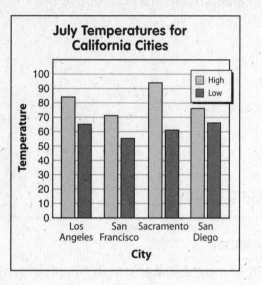

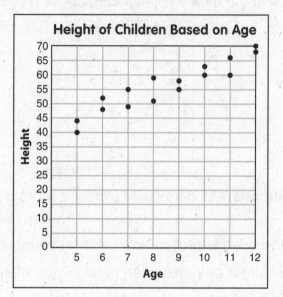

1. Which city has the highest high temperature?

_____

2. Which city has the lowest low temperature?

_____

3. Which city has the smallest difference between high temperature and low temperature?

_____

4. What is the relationship between age and height?

_____

5. What would the scatter plot look like if children got shorter as they got older?

_____

_____

_____

6. If you drew a line through the points on the scatter plot, would the point (6, 60) be on your line? How do you know?

_____

_____

_____

Name _____ Date _____

Hands On: Probability and Outcomes

CA Standards
SDAP 2.0, SDAP 2.2

Write *certain, likely, equally likely, unlikely,* or *impossible* to describe the probability of landing on a shaded area.

> **Step 1** Look at the shaded area of the spinner and compare it to the unshaded area.
>
> **Step 2** Note that half of the wheel is shaded and half is unshaded.
>
> The probability is equally likely.

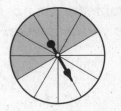

1. _____

2. _____

3. _____

tally chart shows the results of picking colored cards
a bag. The card was replaced after each pick. Use the
for problems 4–5.

it *certain, likely, equally likely, unlikely,*
r *impossible* to pick an orange card?

_____

s it *certain, likely, equally likely, unlikely,*
r *impossible* to pick a yellow card?

_____

Picking Cards		
Outcome	**Tally**	**Number**
Yellow	ＨＨＴ I	6
Orange	ＨＨＴ ＨＨＴ III	13
Green	ＨＨＴ II	7

piral Review (Chapter 18, Lesson 2) **KEY** NS 1.9, NS 1.5

ide whether the fractions are equivalent. Write *yes* or *no.*
fraction tiles to help you.

$\frac{4}{10}$ and $\frac{2}{5}$

7. $\frac{2}{12}$ and $\frac{1}{8}$

_____

_____

8. Helen sliced the cake into 12 slices. She and her friends ate 8 slices. What two fractions express the amount of cake left?

_____

Hands On: Probability and Outcomes

Keesha created the three spinners shown below based on the face of a clock. Use the information from the spinner to solve the problems. Use *certain, likely, equally likely, unlikely,* or *impossible* for your answers.

1   2   3

1. What is the probability of landing on an odd number on the second spinner?

_____

2. What is the probability of landing on odd number on the third spinner?

_____

3. Is it *likely, unlikely,* or *equally likely* to land on an odd number as an even number on the first spinner?

_____

4. Keesha added a 3 and a 9 to the second spinner. What is the probability now of landing on an odd number?

_____

5. Keesha removed 1, 3, and 11 from the first spinner. What is the probability now of landing on an even number?

_____

6. Keesha removed all the numbers except 7 from the third spinner. What is the probability now of landing on 7?

_____

Name _____ Date _____

Find Probability

For each spinner, write the probability that a spin will land on a shaded region. Write the probability in both words and fraction form.

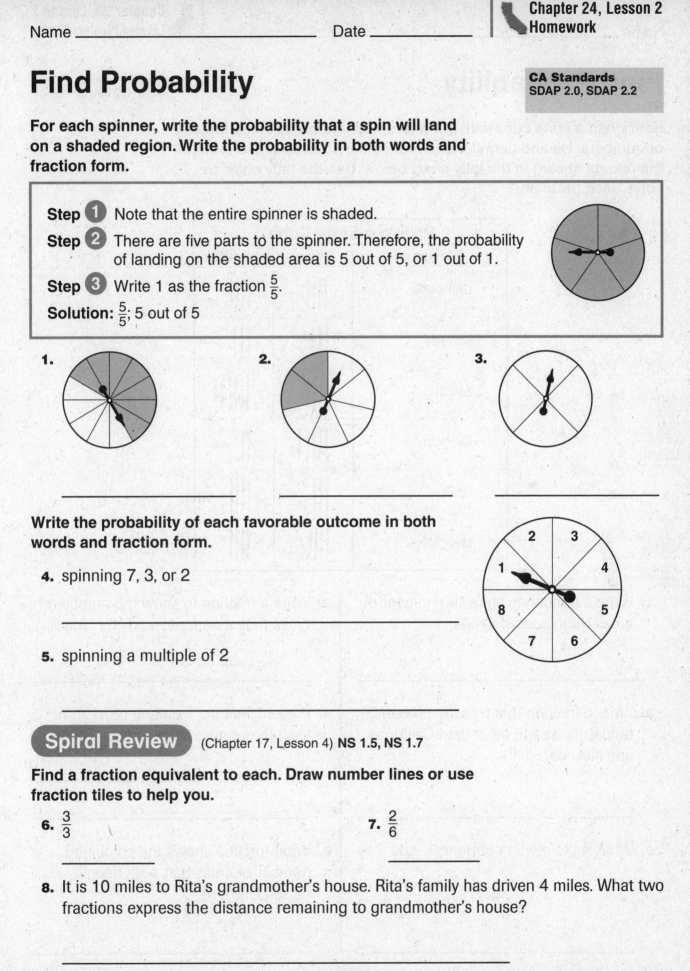

Step 1 Note that the entire spinner is shaded.

Step 2 There are five parts to the spinner. Therefore, the probability of landing on the shaded area is 5 out of 5, or 1 out of 1.

Step 3 Write 1 as the fraction $\frac{5}{5}$.

Solution: $\frac{5}{5}$; 5 out of 5

1. _____

2. _____

3. _____

Write the probability of each favorable outcome in both words and fraction form.

4. spinning 7, 3, or 2

_____

5. spinning a multiple of 2

_____

Spiral Review (Chapter 17, Lesson 4) NS 1.5, NS 1.7

Find a fraction equivalent to each. Draw number lines or use fraction tiles to help you.

6. $\frac{3}{3}$ _____

7. $\frac{2}{6}$ _____

8. It is 10 miles to Rita's grandmother's house. Rita's family has driven 4 miles. What two fractions express the distance remaining to grandmother's house?

_____

Name _____   Date _____

Find Probability

CA Standards
SDAP 2.0 , SDAP 2.2

Henry had a state cube with six western states on its sides instead of numbers. He and Jennifer each rolled the cube 25 times and got the results shown in the tally chart below. Use the tally chart to solve each problem.

Rolling a State Cube		
Outcomes	**Henry**	**Jennifer**
California	IIII	IIII
Nevada	III	III
Arizona	IIII	IIII II
Oregon	IIII	II
Utah	III	IIII
New Mexico	IIII	IIII

1. Write a fraction to show the number of times Henry tossed Oregon.

_____

2. Write a fraction to show the number of times that Jennifer tossed New Mexico.

_____

3. Write a fraction that tells the probability of tossing a state other than California and Nevada.

_____

4. Present Jennifer's data in order from least to greatest. What is the mode?

_____

5. What is the median of Henry's data ?

_____

6. What fraction shows the combined number of times that both people tossed Oregon?

_____

Name _____ Date _____

Make Predictions

CA Standards
SDAP 2.0, SDAP 2.2

A cube has its faces labeled with the following letters: A, B,
C, A, B, A. Use this cube to solve each problem.

> **Predict how many times the cube will land on the letter
> B if you toss the cube 60 times.**
>
> **Step 1** Find the probability of rolling the letter B once.
> Letter B → 2 out of 6 = $\frac{1}{3}$
>
> **Step 2** Predict the number of times the cube will land on letter B.
> Letter B → $\frac{1}{3}$ of 60 = 20 rolls
>
> **Solution:** It is probable that 20 rolls out of 60 rolls will land on the letter B.

1. Predict how many times the cube will land on the letter C if you toss the cube 30 times.

2. Predict how many times the cube will land on the letter A if you toss the cube 20 times.

3. Predict how many times the cube will land on the letter B if you toss the cube 150 times.

4. Suppose one of the faces with an "A" was changed to a "D". Predict how many times the new cube will land on the letter A if you toss it 480 times.

Spiral Review (Chapter 9, Lesson 2) **KEY** AF 1.5, AF 1.1

If $y = 2x$, what is the value of x or y in each case?

5. $y = 4$

6. $x = 3$

7. If there are 12 songs on each CD in a series and the equation is $y = 12x$, how many songs are on 3 of the CDs in this series?

Name _____ Date _____

Make Predictions

CA Standards
SDAP 2.0, SDAP 2.2

The bar graph shows the results of a coin experiment. Each time a coin was picked, it was returned to the bag. Use the graph to solve the problems.

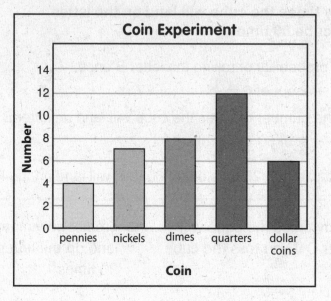

1. How many times was a nickel pulled out of the bag?

_____

2. What coin was pulled out of the bag 12 times?

_____

3. How many more times were dimes pulled out than dollar coins?

_____

4. What was the total number of times coins were pulled from the bag?

_____

5. If there were only 9 coins in the bag, how many quarters and dollar coins do you predict there were?

_____

6. If there were 36 coins in the bag, how many pennies and dimes do you predict there were?

_____

Represent Outcomes

CA Standards
SDAP 2.1, SDAP 2.2

Use the spinner to solve each problem.

If you spin the spinner two times, what is the probability that the spinner will land on the black region twice?	

Step ①

Use a grid to list all possible spins.

Second Spin

First Spin		black	white	striped
	black	black, black	black, white	black, striped
	white	white, black	white, white	white, striped
	striped	striped, black	striped, white	striped, striped

Step ②

Count the number of outcomes that have black two times.

Solution: The probability of landing on black twice is $\frac{1}{9}$ or 1 out of 9.

1. What is the probability of one spin landing on the white area and one spin landing on the black area?

_____

2. What is the probability that one of the spins will land on the white area and that the other will not land on the white area?

_____

Spiral Review (Chapter 23, Lesson 2) **SDAP 1.1, SDAP 1.2**

Find the median and mode in each set of data.

3. 3, 4, 5, 5, 8, 10

_____

4. 16, 21, 25, 38, 38

_____

5. Tracy kept a record of the temperatures in various cities on one day. They were 64, 73, 79, 82, 87, 110. What is the median? What is the outlier?

_____

Represent Outcomes

CA Standards
SDAP 2.1, SDAP 2.2

Many towns and cities hold First Night celebrations on January 1st. Hector's town offers musical and theater events for the public at First Night. Since most of the events are scheduled at the same time, visitors must choose what they will attend. The tree diagram shows the events scheduled for First Night.

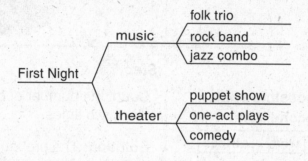

1. How many musical events can Hector choose from?

_____

2. What is the probability that Hector will attend the comedy?

_____

3. What is the probability that Hector and his friends will go to see the folk trio or the puppet show?

_____

4. The rock band has to cancel its performance because one of its members has the flu. What is the probability now of going to the jazz combo?

_____

5. The first night committee adds 2 art exhibits to the schedule of events. What is the probability of attending one of these exhibits, given that there is no rock band?

_____

6. If there are 350 people who attend the First Night celebration and an equal number attend each event as described in 5, how many people attend the one-act plays?

_____

Name _____ Date _____

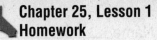
Hands On: Points, Lines, and Line Segments

CA Standards
MG 3.1, MG 3.0

Use words and symbols to name each figure.

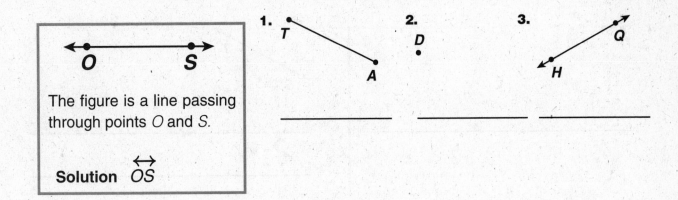

The figure is a line passing through points *O* and *S*.

Solution $\overleftrightarrow{OS}$

1.

T

A

_____

2.

D

_____

3.

Q

H

_____

Write *parallel*, *intersecting*, or *perpendicular* to best describe the relationship between each pair of lines.

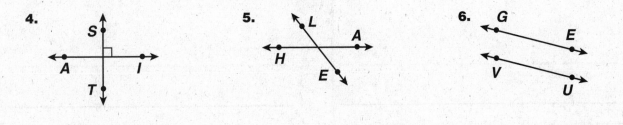

4.

S

A   I

T

_____

5.

L

A

H

E

_____

6.

G

E

V

U

_____

Spiral Review (Chapter 20, Lesson 4) **NS 2.1, NS 2.2**

Add or subtract. Use estimation to check.

7. $3.6 + 6.2 =$

8. $23.7 - 21.4 =$

_____

_____

9. Henry walked 12.5 miles during one week. The next week he walked 7.4 miles. How far did he walk in all?

_____

Hands On: Points, Lines, and Line Segments

CA Standards
MG 3.1, MG 3.0

Use words and symbols to name each figure. If two lines are shown, include the word parallel, intersecting, or perpendicular to describe the relationship between the lines.

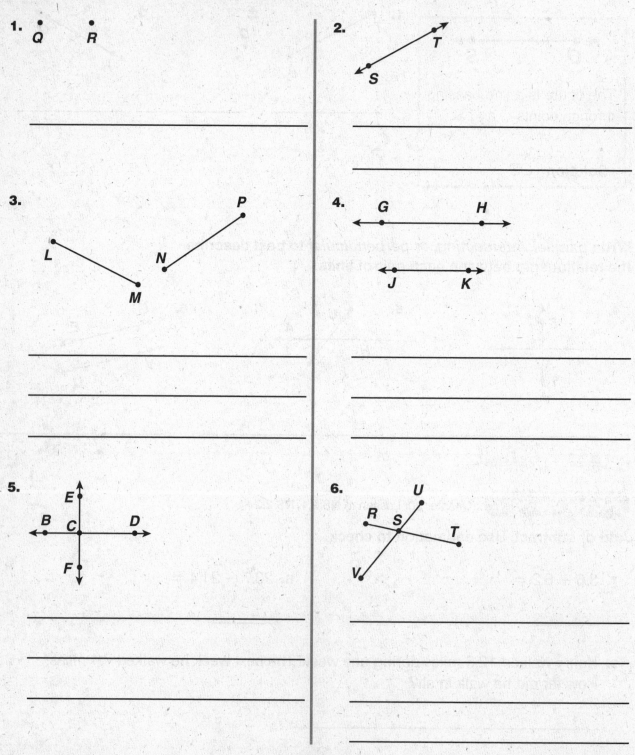

1.

Q   R

_____

2.

T

S

_____

_____

3.

P

L

N

M

_____

_____

4.

G   H

J   K

_____

_____

5.

E

B   C   D

F

_____

_____

6.

U

R   S   T

V

_____

_____

Name _____ Date _____

Rays and Angles

CA Standards
MG 3.5, MG 3.0

Name each angle in three ways. Then classify the angle as
acute, obtuse, or *right*.

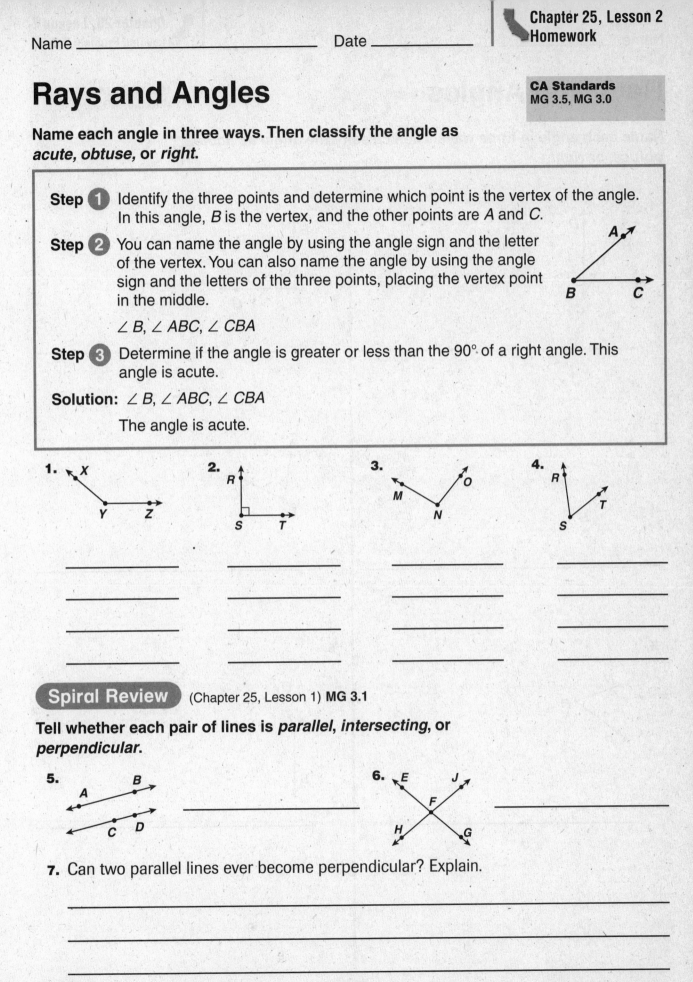

Step 1 Identify the three points and determine which point is the vertex of the angle. In this angle, *B* is the vertex, and the other points are *A* and *C*.

Step 2 You can name the angle by using the angle sign and the letter of the vertex. You can also name the angle by using the angle sign and the letters of the three points, placing the vertex point in the middle.

∠ *B*, ∠ *ABC*, ∠ *CBA*

Step 3 Determine if the angle is greater or less than the 90° of a right angle. This angle is acute.

Solution: ∠ *B*, ∠ *ABC*, ∠ *CBA*

The angle is acute.

1. *X* *Y* *Z*

_____

_____

_____

_____

2. *R* *S* *T*

_____

_____

_____

_____

3. *M* *N* *O*

_____

_____

_____

_____

4. *R* *T* *S*

_____

_____

_____

_____

Spiral Review (Chapter 25, Lesson 1) **MG 3.1**

Tell whether each pair of lines is *parallel, intersecting,* **or**
perpendicular.

5. *A* *B* *C* *D*

_____

6. *E* *J* *F* *H* *G*

_____

7. Can two parallel lines ever become perpendicular? Explain.

_____

_____

_____

Rays and Angles

CA Standards
MG 3.5, MG 3.0

Name each angle in three ways. Then classify the angle as *acute,*
obtuse, or *right.*

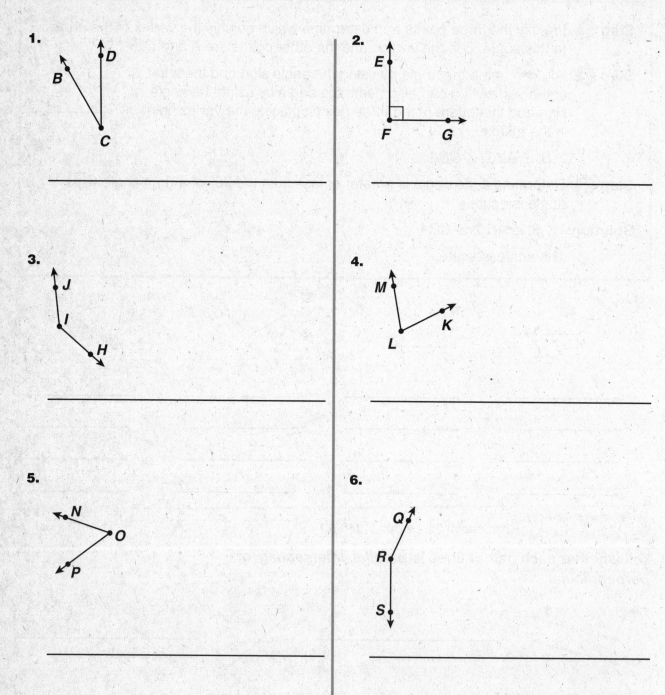

1.

_____

2.

_____

3.

_____

4.

_____

5.

_____

6.

_____

Name _____ Date _____

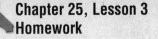
Polygons and Quadrilaterals

CA Standards
MG 3.8, MG 3.0

Name each polygon. If the polygon is a quadrilateral, write all names that apply.

Step 1 Look at the figure to see how many sides it has, the lengths of the sides, and if any of the sides are parallel. This figure has 4 sides. All of the sides are of equal length. Each side is parallel to an opposite side.

Step 2 Remember that a polygon can be a triangle (3 sides), a quadrilateral (4 sides), a pentagon (5 sides), a hexagon (6 sides), or an octagon (8 sides). This figure is a quadrilateral.

Step 3 Also remember that quadrilaterals can have special names because of their characteristics. These include rectangle, square, trapezoid, parallelogram, and rhombus. This figure is a square.

1.

_____

2.

_____

3.

_____

4.

_____

Spiral Review (Chapter 21, Lesson 4) **KEY** MG 2.0, **KEY** MG 2.1

For each equation, make a function table with 10 values. Then graph the equation on a coordinate grid.

5. $x = 12$

6. $y = 3x$

7. How would you graph the equation $y = 2x + 3$?

Polygons and Quadrilaterals

CA Standards
MG 3.8, MG 3.0

Name each polygon. If the polygon is a quadrilateral, write all names that apply.

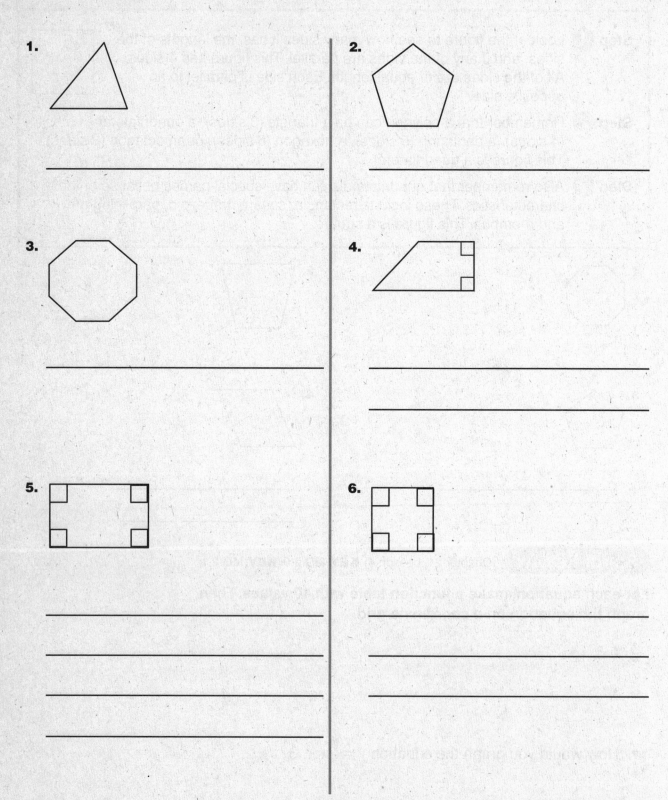

1.

_____

2.

_____

3.

_____

4.

_____

_____

5.

_____

_____

_____

_____

6.

_____

_____

_____

Classify Triangles

CA Standards
MG 3.7, MG 3.0

Tell whether each triangle appears to be *equilateral*, *isosceles*, or *scalene*. Then tell whether each triangle appears to be *right*, *obtuse*, or *acute*.

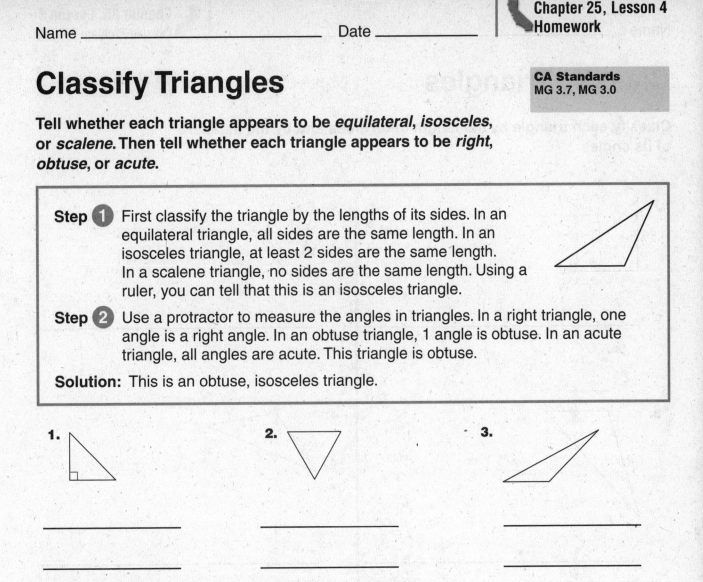

Step 1 First classify the triangle by the lengths of its sides. In an equilateral triangle, all sides are the same length. In an isosceles triangle, at least 2 sides are the same length. In a scalene triangle, no sides are the same length. Using a ruler, you can tell that this is an isosceles triangle.

Step 2 Use a protractor to measure the angles in triangles. In a right triangle, one angle is a right angle. In an obtuse triangle, 1 angle is obtuse. In an acute triangle, all angles are acute. This triangle is obtuse.

Solution: This is an obtuse, isosceles triangle.

1. _____ 2. _____ 3. _____

_____ _____ _____

Draw one example of each triangle described below.

4. an isosceles triangle that is also a right triangle

5. an equilateral triangle that is also an acute triangle

Spiral Review (Chapter 22, Lesson 4) **KEY** MG 2.2, **KEY** MG 2.3

Graph and connect each pair of points. Then count units to find the length of each line segment.

6. (3, −6) (5, −6)

7. (−1, 6) (−1, 9)

8. What is the length of the line segment formed by the point (0, −4) and the point (0, 4)?

Classify Triangles

CA Standards
MG 3.7, MG 3.0

Classify each triangle by the length of its sides and by the measure
of its angles.

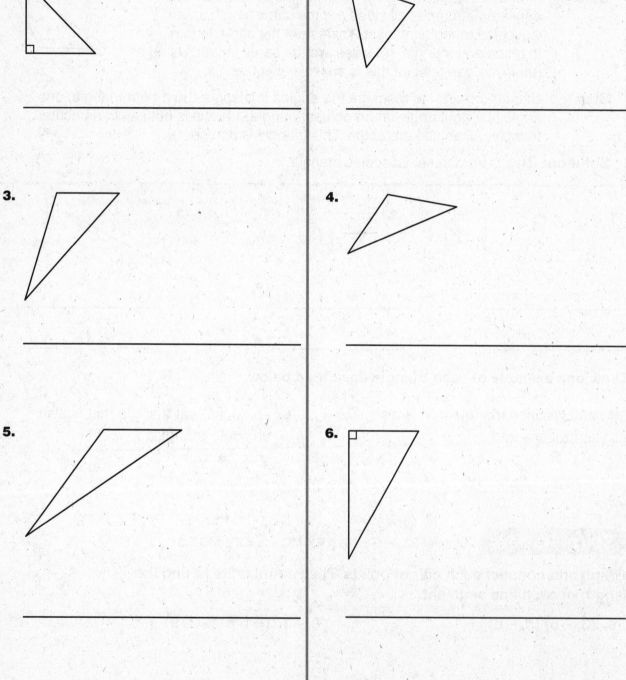

1.

_____

2.

_____

3.

_____

4.

_____

5.

_____

6.

_____

Name _____ Date _____

Circles

CA Standards
MG 3.2, MG 3.5

Name the part of each circle that is given. Write *center*, *radius*, or *diameter*.

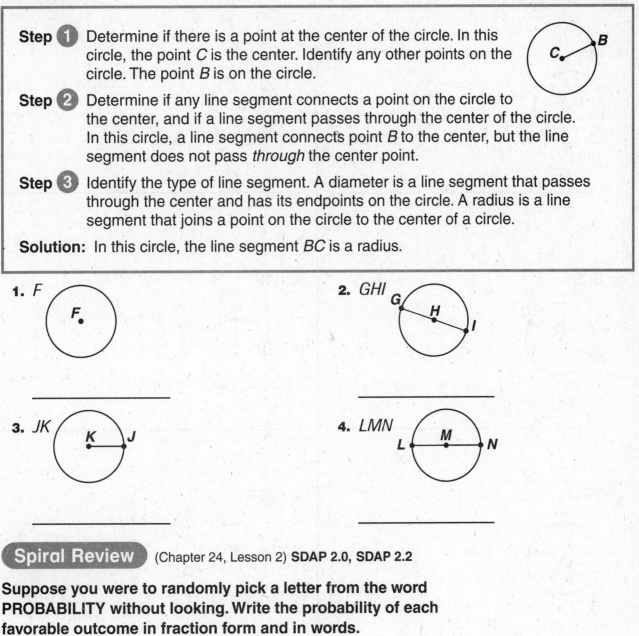

Step 1 Determine if there is a point at the center of the circle. In this circle, the point *C* is the center. Identify any other points on the circle. The point *B* is on the circle.

Step 2 Determine if any line segment connects a point on the circle to the center, and if a line segment passes through the center of the circle. In this circle, a line segment connects point *B* to the center, but the line segment does not pass *through* the center point.

Step 3 Identify the type of line segment. A diameter is a line segment that passes through the center and has its endpoints on the circle. A radius is a line segment that joins a point on the circle to the center of a circle.

Solution: In this circle, the line segment *BC* is a radius.

1. *F*

_____

2. *GHI*

_____

3. *JK*

_____

4. *LMN*

_____

Spiral Review (Chapter 24, Lesson 2) **SDAP 2.0, SDAP 2.2**

Suppose you were to randomly pick a letter from the word PROBABILITY without looking. Write the probability of each favorable outcome in fraction form and in words.

5. R

6. I

7. Terry and Jamaal have shuffled a deck of 52 cards. The deck contains 13 clubs, 13 diamonds, 13 spades, and 13 hearts. Without looking at the faces of the cards, Terry selects a card from the middle of the deck. What is the probability that she has chosen a heart? Write the probability in fraction form and in words.

Circles

CA Standards
MG 3.2, MG 3.5

Name of the part of each circle that is given. Write *center*,
radius, or *diameter*.

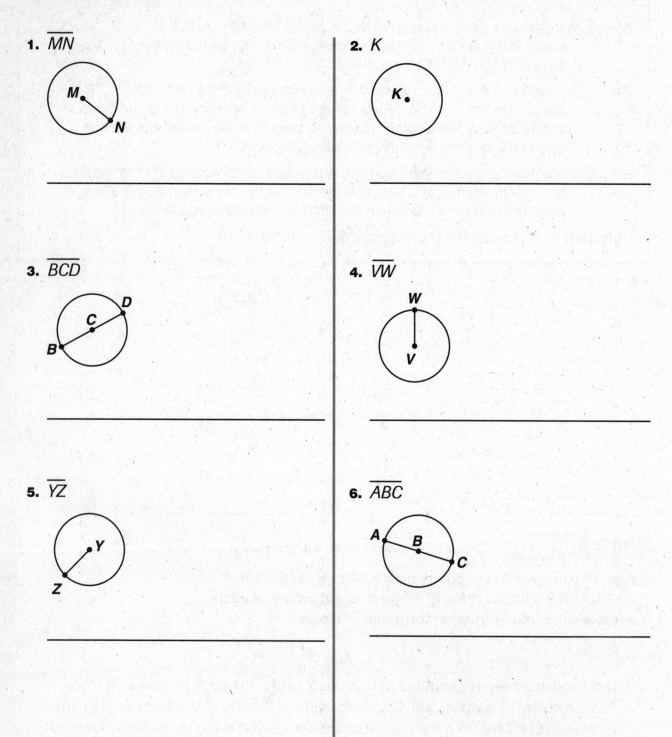

1. $\overline{MN}$

_____

2. K

_____

3. $\overline{BCD}$

_____

4. $\overline{VW}$

_____

5. $\overline{YZ}$

_____

6. $\overline{ABC}$

_____

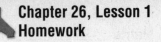
Hands On: Line Symmetry

Is the dashed line a line of symmetry? Write *yes* or *no*.

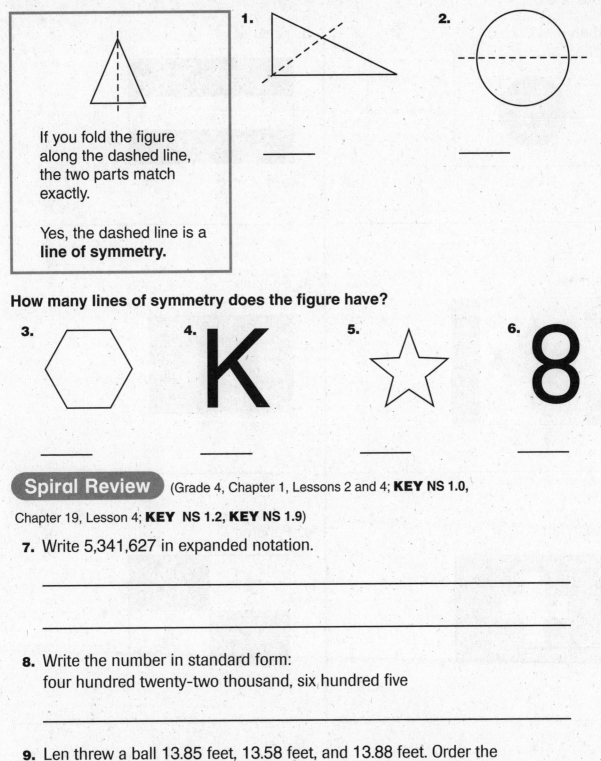

If you fold the figure along the dashed line, the two parts match exactly.

Yes, the dashed line is a **line of symmetry.**

1. _____

2. _____

How many lines of symmetry does the figure have?

3. _____

4. K _____

5. ☆ _____

6. 8 _____

Spiral Review (Grade 4, Chapter 1, Lessons 2 and 4; **KEY** NS 1.0,

Chapter 19, Lesson 4; **KEY** NS 1.2, **KEY** NS 1.9)

7. Write 5,341,627 in expanded notation.

_____

_____

8. Write the number in standard form:
four hundred twenty-two thousand, six hundred five

_____

9. Len threw a ball 13.85 feet, 13.58 feet, and 13.88 feet. Order the
distances from greatest to least.

_____

Hands On: Line Symmetry

**Look at the flag. Write how many lines of symmetry it has.
Draw the lines.**

1. Japan

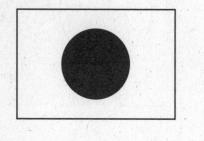

_____

2. Austria

_____

3. Canada

_____

4. Somalia

_____

5. Switzerland

_____

6. Panama

_____

Name _____ Date _____

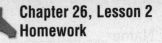

Line or Bilateral Symmetry

CA Standards
MG 3.0, MG 3.4

Is the dashed line a line of symmetry? Write *yes* or *no*.

If you fold the figure along the dashed line, the two parts match exactly. The dashed line is a **line of symmetry**.

Does the dashed line identify a line of symmetry for the figure?

1.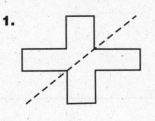

_____

2.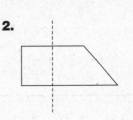

_____

How many lines of symmetry does the figure have?

3. 4. 5. 6.

_____ _____ _____ _____

Spiral Review (Chapter 25, Lesson 2) MG 3.5, MG 3.0

Name each angle in three ways and classify it as *acute*, *obtuse*, or *right*.

7.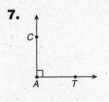

8.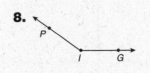

9. It is 11:00. What kind of angle do the hands of a clock make?

_____ _____ _____

Line or Bilateral Symmetry

The Greek alphabet uses different letters than our alphabet.

How many lines of symmetry does each Greek letter have? Write the number and draw the line or lines.

1. pi (letter p)

Π

_____

2. omega (letter o)

Ω

_____

3. phi (sound ph/f)

Φ

_____

4. psi (sound ps)

Ψ

_____

5. gamma (letter g)

Γ

_____

6. theta (sound th)

Θ

_____

Name _____ Date _____

Rotational Symmetry

CA Standards
MG 3.4, MG 3.5

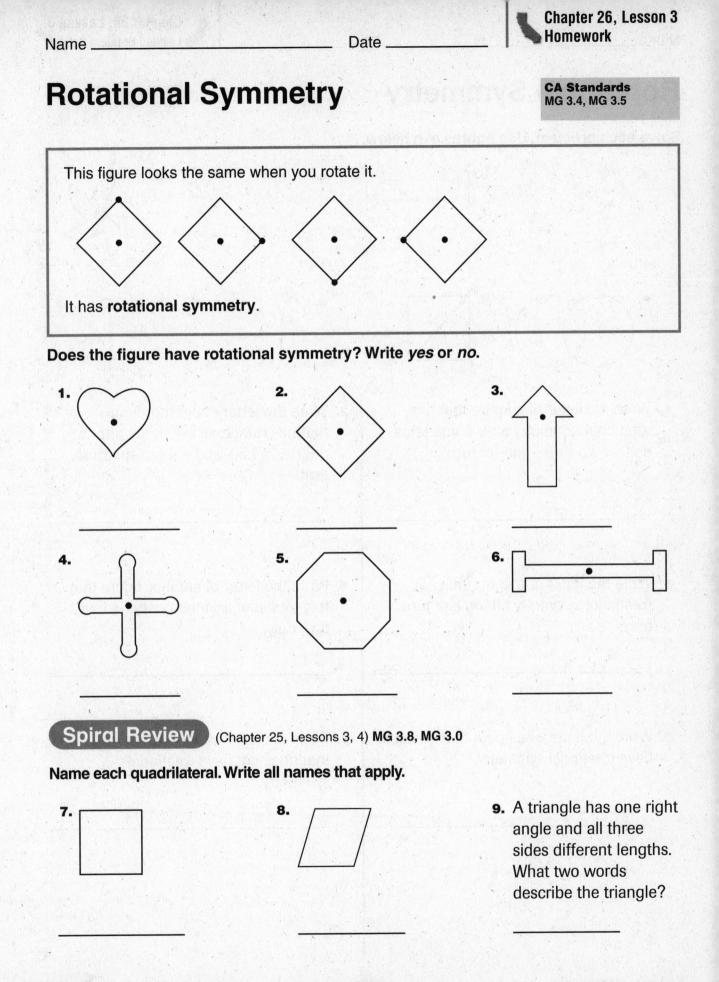

This figure looks the same when you rotate it.

It has **rotational symmetry**.

Does the figure have rotational symmetry? Write *yes* or *no*.

1. _____

2. _____

3. _____

4. _____

5. _____

6. _____

Spiral Review (Chapter 25, Lessons 3, 4) **MG 3.8, MG 3.0**

Name each quadrilateral. Write all names that apply.

7. _____

8. _____

9. A triangle has one right angle and all three sides different lengths. What two words describe the triangle?

_____

Rotational Symmetry

CA Standards
MG 3.4, MG 3.5

Solve each problem. Use figures a–h below.

a. 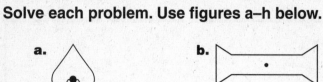   **b.** 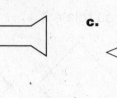   **c.**    **d.**

e. 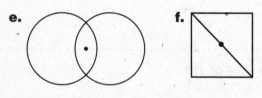   **f.**   **g.**   **h.**

1. Write the letter of a figure that has rotational symmetry after a quarter, a half, and a three-quarter turn.

_____

2. Write the letter of another figure that has rotational symmetry after a quarter, a half, and a three-quarter turn.

_____

3. Write the letter of a figure that has rotational symmetry after a half turn only.

_____

4. Write the letter of another figure that has rotational symmetry after a half turn only.

_____

5. Write the letter of a figure that does not have rotational symmetry.

_____

6. Write the letter of another figure that does not have rotational symmetry.

_____

Congruent Figures

Do the figures in each pair appear to be congruent?
Write *yes* or *no*.

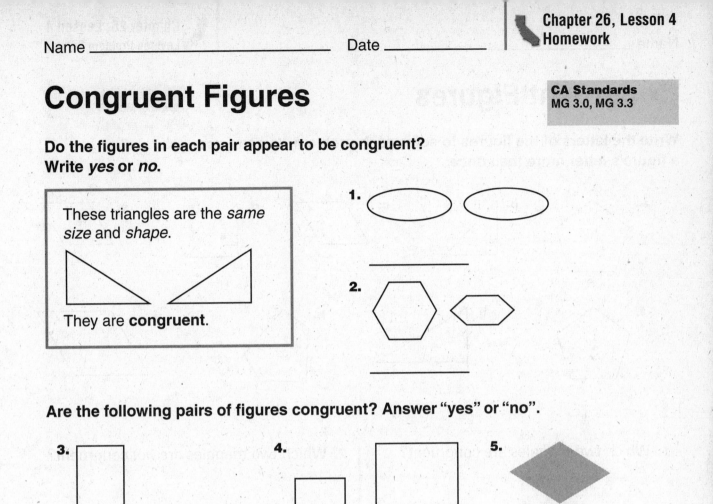

These triangles are the *same size* and *shape*.

They are **congruent**.

1. _____

2. _____

_____

Are the following pairs of figures congruent? Answer "yes" or "no".

3. _____

4. _____

5. _____

Spiral Review (Chapter 23, Lesson 3) SDAP 1.3, SDAP 1.0

Use the graph to answer the questions.

6. How much more snow did Buffalo have than
   Corning in February? _____ inches

7. How much more snow did Buffalo have in all?
   _____ inches

8. In March, it snowed 4 inches in Corning and
   0 inches in Buffalo. Now which city had more snow
   in all? What is the difference in the total inches?

_____

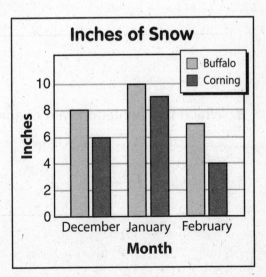

Inches of Snow

Buffalo
Corning

Congruent Figures

Write the letters of the figures to solve each problem. You can use a figure's letter more than once.

a. b. c. d. e.

f. g. h. i.

1. Which two triangles are congruent?

_____

2. Which two triangles are *not* congruent?

_____

3. Which two rhombuses are congruent?

_____

4. Which two rhombuses are *not* congruent?

_____

5. Which two pentagons are congruent?

_____

6. Which two pentagons are *not* congruent?

_____

Name _____ Date _____

Problem Solving: Patterns in the Coordinate Grid

CA Standards
MR 1.1, MG 3.0

Example:
The congruent squares form a pattern on the coordinate grid. If the pattern continues, what are the ordered pairs for the vertices of the fourth square?

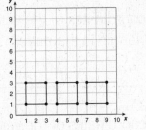

You want to find the ordered pairs for the vertices of the next square in the pattern.

Look at the coordinates of the bottom-left vertex for each square.

Square	1	2	3	4
X	1	4	7	☐
Y	1	1	1	☐

Look at the coordinates of the top-left vertex for each square.

Square	1	2	3	4
X	1	4	7	☐
Y	3	3	3	☐

Look at the coordinates of the bottom-right vertex for each square.

Square	1	2	3	4
X	3	6	9	☐
Y	1	1	1	☐

Look at the coordinates of the top-right vertex for each square.

Square	1	2	3	4
X	3	6	9	☐
Y	3	3	3	☐

For each vertex, the x-value is increased by 3 in each successive square.
Thus the coordinates of the vertices for the fourth square are:
(10, 1), (10, 3), (12, 1) and (12, 3).

1. Continue the pattern above to find the coordinates of the fifth square in the pattern.

_____

2. Find the coordinates of the vertices of the fourth triangle in the pattern below.

_____

Problem Solving: Patterns in the Coordinate Grid

CA Standards
MR 1.1, MG 3.0

Use the pattern below to solve problems 1–3.

1. What are the coordinates of the vertices of the fourth triangle in the pattern?

   _____

2. What are the coordinates of the vertices of the fifth triangle in the pattern?

   _____

3. Daryl continued the pattern until he got a triangle with vertices (22, 2), (22, 3), (23, 2). How many triangles did he draw before getting this triangle?

   _____

   _____

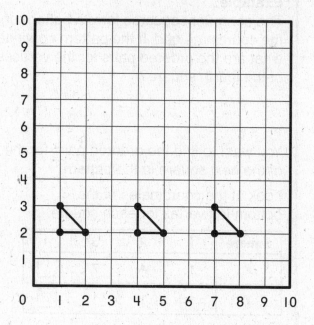

Use the pattern below to solve problems 4–6.

4. What is the pattern?

   _____

   _____

   _____

5. How many rectangles were drawn to obtain the coordinates (27, 9), (27, 12), (30, 9), (30, 12)?

   _____

6. What are the coordinates of the 17th rectangle in the sequence?

   _____

   _____

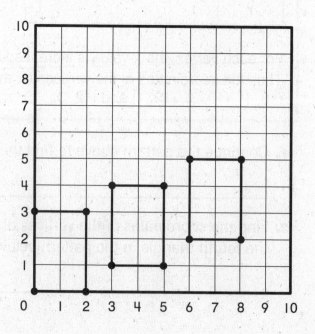

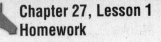
Hands On: Model Perimeter and Area

CA Standards
MG 1.2, MG 1.3

Solve.

> **Do the rectangles have the same perimeter? Do they have the same area?**
>
> 5 units
> 2 units
>
> 4 units
> 3 units
>
> **Find the perimeter and area of each rectangle.**
>
> | Length | Width | Perimeter | Area |
> |--------|-------|-----------|------|
> | 5 units | 2 units | 14 units | 10 square units |
> | 4 units | 3 units | 14 unts | 12 square units |
>
> **Solution:** The rectangles have the same perimeter but not the same area.

1. Draw two rectangles with the same areas but which different perimeters.

2. Draw two rectangles with different areas but the same perimeter.

Spiral Review   (Chapter 23 Lesson 4) **SDAP 1.0, SDAP 1.3**

Use the line graph to answer the questions.

3. What was the lowest number of lunches sold?

_____

4. On what days were the same number of lunches sold?

_____

5. Were the most lunches sold early or late in the week?

_____

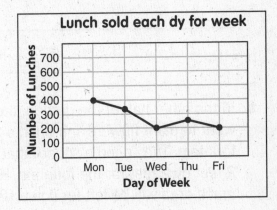

Lunch sold each dy for week

Hands On: Model Perimeter and Area

CA Standards
MG 1.2, MG 1.3

Solve each problem.

1. Terry is helping his parents draw a plan for a garden. They are planning a garden shaped like a rectangle with sides of 6 feet and 12 feet. Draw an outline of the garden on the grid.

2. What is the total area of the planned garden?

_____

3. Terry's dad bought 2 rolls of fencing to go around the garden. Each roll is 20 feet long. Will they have enough fence to go around all four sides of the garden? Explain your answer.

_____

_____

_____

4. They plan to plant vegetables in half of the garden. How much of the area will be used for vegetables?

_____

_____

5. In the other half of the garden, they want to plant flowers and build a fountain. They need a square that is 2 feet by 2 feet for the fountain. How much area will be left for flowers?

_____

6. Use the grid to draw their plan for the garden. Put the fountain in the center of the half that has the flowers. Put the vegetables in the other half. Label your drawing.

Use with text pp. 600–601

Name _____ Date _____

Use Formulas for Perimeter

CA Standards
MG 1.4, AF 1.4

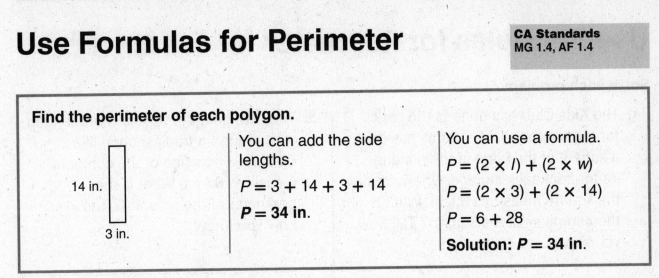

Find the perimeter of each polygon.

You can add the side lengths.

$P = 3 + 14 + 3 + 14$

$P = 34$ in.

You can use a formula.

$P = (2 \times l) + (2 \times w)$

$P = (2 \times 3) + (2 \times 14)$

$P = 6 + 28$

Solution: $P = 34$ in.

Find the perimeter of each polygon.

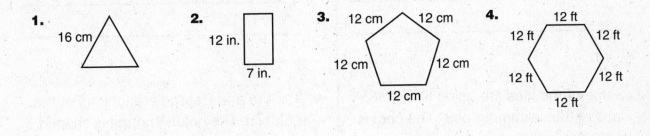

1. 16 cm

2. 12 in. / 7 in.

3. 12 cm, 12 cm, 12 cm, 12 cm, 12 cm

4. 12 ft, 12 ft, 12 ft, 12 ft, 12 ft, 12 ft

_____   _____   _____   _____

Spiral Review   (Chapter 23 Lesson 4) **SDAP 1.0, SDAP 1.3**

Use the line graph to answer the questions.

5. What was the highest amount of snow?

_____

6. During what two months did it snow the least?

_____

7. How much did it snow in six months?

_____

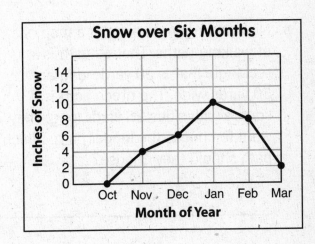

Snow over Six Months

Use with text pp. 602–603

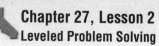
Use Formulas for Perimeter

Solve each problem.

1. The Kids Club has gone to the park for the afternoon. Mrs. Sams has drawn a square at the edge of the parking lot for backpack storage. One side of the square measures 3 feet. What is the perimeter of the square? Tell how you know.

   _____
   _____
   _____

2. They are going to have a three-legged race around a track shaped like an octagon. Each side of the octagon measures 6 feet. What is the perimeter of the octagon? Tell how you know.

   _____
   _____
   _____

3. Some of the kids are going to swim laps in the swimming pool. The pool is a rectangle that is 20 feet wide and 50 feet long. What is the perimeter of the pool? Tell how you know.

   _____
   _____

4. Tamara and George are looking at the goldfish. The goldfish pond is shaped like a triangle. One side is 3 meters long. Another side is 5 meters long. And the third side is 7 meters long. If they walk all the way around the pond, how far will they walk? Tell how you know.

   _____
   _____
   _____

5. Nick and Al are looking at a map of walking paths. The red path is a rectangle that is 30 yards long and 50 yards wide. The green path is square with sides 25 yards long. They want to choose the longer path. Which path should they choose?

   _____
   _____
   _____

6. The perimeter of the walking path sign is 10 feet. It is 2 feet wide. How long is it? Tell how you know.

   _____
   _____

Name _____ Date _____

Use Formulas for Area

Find the area of each figure.

	You can draw a model and count the squares.	You can use a formula.
3 in. ☐ 5 in.	3 in. ⊞ 5 in. $A = 15$ squre feet $A = 15$ ft²	$A = $ length × width $A = l \times w$ $A = 5 \times 3$ $A = 15$ squre feet **Solution:** $A = 15$ ft²

Find the area of each figure.

1.
13 in.
4 in.

_____

2.
15 ft
7 ft

_____

3.
20 cm
8 cm

_____

Find the perimeter and area for each rectangle.

4. 9 yd long, 11 yd wide

5. 14 ft long, 9 ft wide

6. 18 cm long, 6 cm wide

_____   _____   _____

_____   _____   _____

Spiral Review (Chapter 26, Lesson 2) **MG 3.4, MG 3.0**

Is the dashsed line a line of symmetry? Write *yes* or *no*.

7.

8.

9. How many lines of symmetry does the figure have?

Name _____   Date _____

Use Formulas for Areas

CA Standards
MG 1.4, AF 1.4

Solve each problem.

1. Mr. Lee has a square patio. The length of one side of the patio is 8 feet. What is the area of the patio?

   _____

2. The walkway to Mr. Lee's patio is 2 feet wide by 12 feet long. What is the area of the walkway?

   _____

3. Mr. Lee wants to cover the patio and the walkway with stone tiles. If he uses tiles that are 1-foot squares, how many tiles will he need?

   _____

4. If he uses tiles that are 2-foot squares, how many tiles will he need to cover the walkway and the patio?

   _____

5. A new sandlot is being built at the park. The sandlot will be a rectangle. The area of the sandlot will be 60 square feet. The sandlot will be 12 feet long. How wide will the sandlot be?

   _____

6. The practice court at the park is a rectangle. Its width is exactly twice its length. The area of the practice field is 450 ft². What are the length and width of the rectangle?

   _____

   _____

   _____

Leveled Problem Solving
248
Use with text pp. 604–606

Name _____   Date _____

Perimeter and Area of Complex Figures

CA Standards
MG 1.4, AF 1.4

Find the area of each figure.

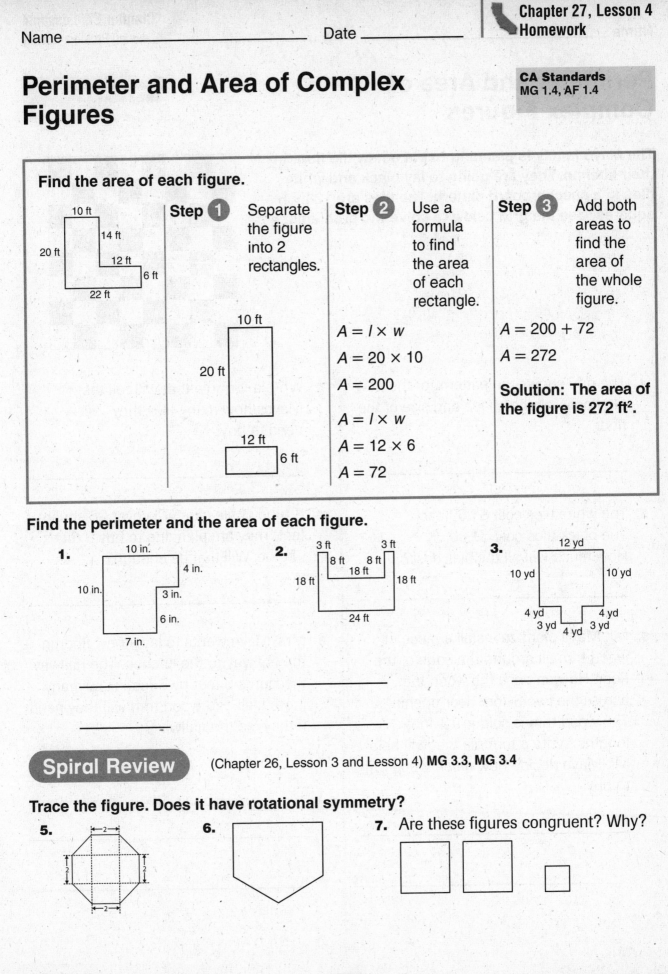

Step 1 Separate the figure into 2 rectangles.

Step 2 Use a formula to find the area of each rectangle.

$A = l \times w$
$A = 20 \times 10$
$A = 200$

$A = l \times w$
$A = 12 \times 6$
$A = 72$

Step 3 Add both areas to find the area of the whole figure.

$A = 200 + 72$
$A = 272$

Solution: The area of the figure is 272 ft².

Find the perimeter and the area of each figure.

1.

2.

3.

_____   _____   _____

_____   _____   _____

Spiral Review   (Chapter 26, Lesson 3 and Lesson 4) **MG 3.3, MG 3.4**

Trace the figure. Does it have rotational symmetry?

5.

6.

7. Are these figures congruent? Why?

Name _____   Date _____

Perimeter and Area of Complex Figures

CA Standards
MG 1.4, AF 1.4

The Mayo family is planning to put a new tile floor in their kitchen. They are going to lay black and white tiles in a checkerboard pattern. The tiles are 12-inch squares. Use the grid below to solve the problems.

1. The grid shows the pattern for the new tile floor. Tell the shape and size of the floor.

   _____

2. Write a formula that will tell the Mayos how many tiles they need to buy.

   _____

3. The white tiles cost $1.60 each. The black tiles cost $1.80. How much will all the tiles cost?

   _____

4. A tube of tile glue will cover 25 square feet. They are planning to buy 3 tubes of glue. Will that be enough?

   _____

5. Mr. Mayo plans to install a piece of wood trim all around the edge of the floor. He won't use the wood trim across the two 3-foot door openings. The wood trim is sold in 12-foot lengths. Write a formula that will help Mr. Mayo decide how much wood trim to buy.

   _____

   _____

6. Mrs. Mayo wants to lay a new floor in the hallway to the kitchen. The hallway measures 3 feet by 5 feet. How many more tiles and wood trim will they need if they tile the hallway?

   _____

   _____

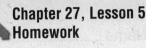
Problem Solving: Use Formulas

CA Standards
MR 2.3, AF 1.4

Use a formula to solve.

Lars has a storage trunk that is 4 feet long, 2 feet high, and 3 feet wide. He wants to paint a border around the edges of the front panel of the trunk. How long will the border be?

Find the perimeter of the front panel. Use the formula for the perimeter of a rectangle.

$P = (2 \times l) + (2 \times w)$

$P = (2 \times 2) + (2 \times 3)$

$P = 4 + 6$

$P = 10$ ft.

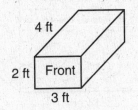

The border will be 10 feet long.

A closet in Matt's house is 3 feet long, 3 feet wide and 8 feet high.

1. What is the area of the floor of the closet? _____

2. If Matt were to put a border around the floor of the closet,

   how long would the border be? _____

3. How many square feet of wallpaper would you need to cover

   the back and sides of the closet? _____

Spiral Review   (Chapter 21, Lesson 3) **KEY** MG 2.0, **KEY** MG 2.1

4. What is the function rule for the table?

   _____

5. Plot the points in the table on a coordinate grid.

   _____

x	y
2	4
3	6
4	8
5	10

6. Use the graph and the function rule to determine the value of y if $x = 12$.

   _____

Problem Solving: Use Formulas

Triska is filling the box shown at right with balls. Each ball has a
diameter of 1 cm.

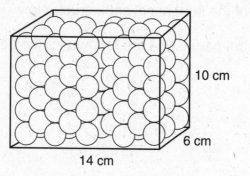

10 cm

6 cm

14 cm

1. How many balls will fit on the bottom
of the box?

_____

2. If you were to fill the box with rows of
balls, how many rows deep would the
box be?

_____

3. How many balls will fit inside the entire
box?

_____

4. What if the width of the box were 5 cm
instead of 6. How would this change
your answer to problem 3?

_____

_____

5. If you were to glue balls all over the
outer surface of the box, how many
balls would you use?

_____

6. About how many of the balls inside the
box do not touch the inside faces of the
box at all?

_____

_____

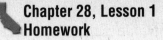
Name _____ Date _____

Hands On: Use Nets to Build Solid Figures

CA Standards
MG 3.6, MR 2.3

Label the drawing.

A net is a pattern you can use to make a solid figure. You cut along the solid lines and fold along the dotted lines.

All the flat parts of a solid figure are called faces.

The line where two faces meet is called an edge.

The point where three edges meet is called a vertex.

Name the solid figure that can be made with the net.

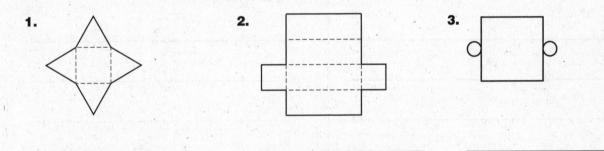

1. _____ 2. _____ 3. _____

Spiral Review (Chapter 27, Lesson 2) **KEY** AF 1.4, MG 1.4

Write a formula to find the perimeter. Then solve.

4. a regular pentagon with sides 4 cm long

5. a hexagon with sides 5 in. long

_____ _____

6. A rectangular flower bed is 3 feet long and 8 feet wide. How many feet of fence will be needed to fence the flower bed?

_____

Hands On: Use Nets to Build Solid Figures

CA Standards
MG 3.6, MR 2.3

Solve each problem.

1. I am a solid figure. All six of my faces are squares. What am I?

_____

2. I am a solid figure. One of my faces has four equal sides. My other four faces are triangles. What am I?

_____

3. Mario has written this description of a triangular prism: *I am a solid figure. Two of my faces are triangles. I have four faces, nine edges, and five vertices.* Is something wrong in Mario's description? Explain your answer.

_____

_____

_____

4. Leo has written this description of a rectangular prism: *I am a solid figure. Four of my faces are squares and two of my faces are rectangles.* Is something wrong in Leo's description? Explain your answer.

_____

_____

_____

_____

5. I am a solid figure. One of my faces has three sides. My other three faces are triangles. What am I?

_____

6. I am a solid figure. Two of my faces have eight equal sides in all. My other four faces are rectangles. What am I?

_____

Use with text pp. 620–621

Solid Figures

Name the solid figure each objects looks like.

The figure has no faces. It is not made up of polygons.

1.

_____

2. Crackers

_____

Name the solid figure that can be made with each net.

3.

_____

4.

_____

5.

_____

Spiral Review (Chapter 27, Lessons 2 and 3) **MG 1.4, AF 1.4**

Write a formula to find the perimeter and area of the rectangle. Then solve.

6. 8 yd long, 6 yd wide

_____

_____

_____

7. 14 cm long, 4 cm wide

_____

_____

_____

8. Mrs. Thomas' dining room is 15 feet long and 12 feet wide. How many square feet of carpet will she need to carpet the entire room?

_____

Name _____ Date _____

Solid Figures

CA Standards
MG 3.0 MG 3.6

Melinda and Cara are sorting solid figures. They have made the
following table. Help them complete the table by writing in the
names of the solid figures. Some solid figures may belong in more
than one box on the table.

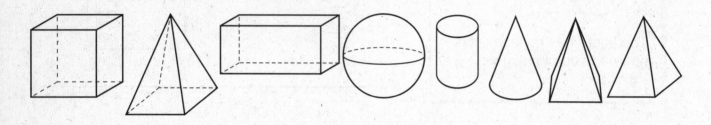

solid figure with all square faces	1. _____ _____ _____
solid figures with all flat faces	2. _____ _____ _____
solid figure that has no flat face	3. _____ _____ _____
solid figures that can roll	4. _____ _____ _____
solid figures that have a *tip*	5. _____ _____ _____
solid figures that have both curved and flat surfaces	6. _____ _____ _____

Name _____ Date _____

Surface Area

CA Standards
MG 1.1, MG 1.4

Find the surface area of this rectangular prism.

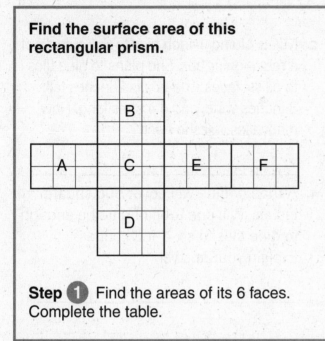

Face	length × width = area
A	3 cm × 2 cm = 6 cm²
B	3 cm × 3 cm = 9 cm²
C	3 cm × 2 cm = 6 cm²
D	3 cm × 3 cm = 9 cm²
E	3 cm × 2 cm = 6 cm²
F	3 cm × 2 cm = 6 cm²

Step 2 Add the areas of the faces to find the surface area of the rectangular prism.

6 cm² + 9 cm² + 6 cm² + 9 cm² + 6 cm² + 6 cm² = surface area of rectangular prism

Solution: 42 cm²

Step 1 Find the areas of its 6 faces. Complete the table.

Use the net to find the surface area of the solid figure.

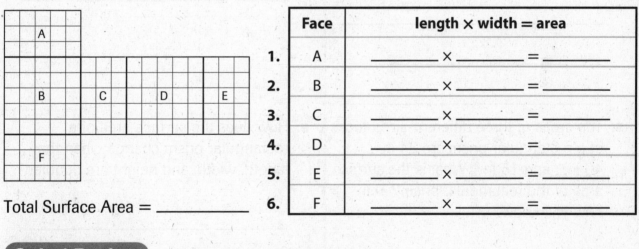

	Face	length × width = area
1.	A	_____ × _____ = _____
2.	B	_____ × _____ = _____
3.	C	_____ × _____ = _____
4.	D	_____ × _____ = _____
5.	E	_____ × _____ = _____
6.	F	_____ × _____ = _____

Total Surface Area = _____

Spiral Review (Chapter 27, Lesson 4) **MG 1.4, AF 1.4**

Find the area. Show the formulas you use.

7.

_____

_____

Surface Area

Solve each problem.

1. A cube has edges that measure 6 inches. What is the surface area of the cube?

_____

2. Mia is gluing 1-inch tiles to the outside of a rectangular box. She plans to glue tiles to all six faces. The box is 2 inches tall, 3 inches wide, and 4 inches long. How many tiles will she need?

_____

3. Ross and Mick are also gluing 1-inch tiles to the outside of rectangular boxes. Ross's box is 3 inches tall, 3 inches wide, and 3 inches long. Mick's box is 4 inches tall, 2 inches wide, and 2 inches long. Who will use more tiles? How many more?

_____

_____

_____

4. A tube of glue will cover 500 square inches. Will one tube of glue be enough to glue tiles to six 4-inch cubes? Explain your answer.

_____

_____

_____

5. The areas of three different-sized faces of a rectangular prism are 24 in.^{2}, 40 in.^{2}, and 15 in.^{2}. What is the surface area of the rectangular prism? Tell how you know.

_____

_____

_____

_____

6. How does the surface area of a rectangular prism change when the length, width, and height are doubled?

_____

_____

Volume

CA Standards
AF 1.4, MG 3.0

Find the volume of each figure.

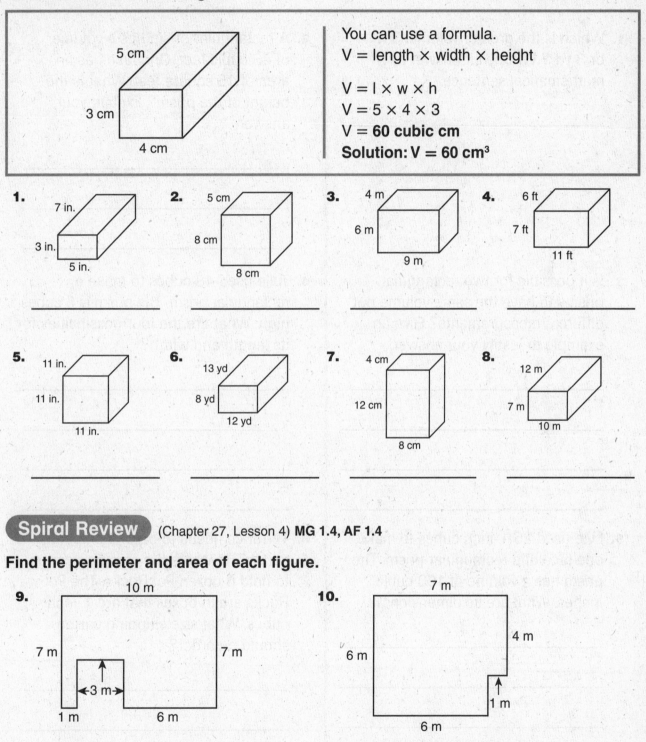

You can use a formula.
V = length × width × height

V = l × w × h
V = 5 × 4 × 3
V = **60 cubic cm**
Solution: V = 60 cm³

1. 7 in. 3 in. 5 in.

_____

2. 5 cm 8 cm 8 cm

_____

3. 4 m 6 m 9 m

_____

4. 6 ft 7 ft 11 ft

_____

5. 11 in. 11 in. 11 in.

_____

6. 13 yd 8 yd 12 yd

_____

7. 4 cm 12 cm 8 cm

_____

8. 12 m 7 m 10 m

_____

Spiral Review (Chapter 27, Lesson 4) **MG 1.4, AF 1.4**

Find the perimeter and area of each figure.

9. 10 m 7 m 7 m 3 m 1 m 6 m

_____
_____
_____
_____

10. 7 m 4 m 6 m 1 m 6 m

_____
_____
_____
_____

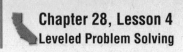
Volume

CA Standards
AF 1.4, MG 3.0

Solve each problem.

1. Which is the greater volume: 3 ft³ or 3 yd³? Write your answer as a mathematical sentence.

_____

2. A rectangular prism has a volume of 45 cubic feet. One face has an area of 15 square feet. What is the height of the prism? Explain your answer.

_____

_____

_____

3. Is it possible for two rectangular prisms to have the same volume but different measurements? Give an example to justify your answer.

_____

_____

_____

4. Julie used 48 cubes to make a rectangular prism. The prism is 6 cubes high. What are the four possibilities for its length and width?

_____

_____

_____

5. Evie used 25 1-inch cubes to make one face of a rectangular prism. The prism has a volume of 100 cubic inches. What are its dimensions?

_____

_____

_____

6. Terrance needs to order a shipping carton. He wants the shipping carton to hold 6 dozen Pet Rocks. The Pet Rocks are in boxes that are 1-inch cubes. What size shipping carton should he order?

_____

_____

_____

Name _____ Date _____

Problem Solving: Surface Area or Volume

CA Standards
MG 3.0, MR 1.0

Example:

Jessica is comparing two boxes. She knows that both boxes have the same volume of 512 ft³. Do they have the same surface area?

Box A — 8 Feet, 8 Feet, 8 Feet

Box B — 8 Feet, 16 Feet, 4 Feet

Find the surface areas of each box to determine if they are equal or not.

Surface Area for Box A

A: $8 \times 8 = 64$ ft²

B: $8 \times 8 = 64$ ft²

C: $8 \times 8 = 64$ ft²

D: $8 \times 8 = 64$ ft²

E: $8 \times 8 = 64$ ft²

F: $8 \times 8 = 64$ ft²

$64 + 64 + 64 + 64 + 64 + 64 = 384$ ft²

Surface Area for Box B

A: $16 \times 4 = 64$ ft²

B: $16 \times 4 = 64$ ft²

C: $16 \times 8 = 128$ ft²

D: $16 \times 8 = 128$ ft²

E: $8 \times 4 = 32$ ft²

F: $8 \times 4 = 32$ ft²

$64 + 64 + 128 + 128 + 32 + 32 = 448$ ft²

The surface area of Box B is greater than the surface area of Box A.

1. What is the surface area of a box that is 3 ft × 4 ft × 5 ft? _____

2. What is the volume of a box that is a 5 ft cube? _____

3. What is the surface area of a box that is 2 ft × 3 ft × 4 ft? _____

Spiral Review (Chapter 16, Lesson 2) **KEY** NS 1.8, NS 1.1
(Chapter 19, Lesson 4) **KEY** NS 1.9, **KEY** NS 1.2

Fill in the box with >, < or =.

4. -2.5 ☐ -1.8

5. 4.81 ☐ 4.79

6. On a winter day, the temperature in St. Petersburg is $-2°F$ and the temperature in Toronto is $-1°F$. Which city is colder?

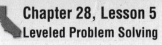
Problem Solving: Surface Area or Volume

Find the volume and surface area.

1.

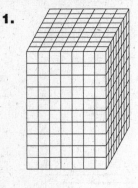

Volume = _____

Surface Area = _____

2.

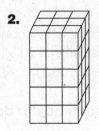

Volume = _____

Surface Area = _____

Determine if the situation requires surface area or volume to solve.

3. Alex wants to know how much gift wrap to use to wrap a box. Surface Area or Volume?

_____

4. Kai needs to measure a box to see how many tennis balls it can hold. Surface Area or Volume?

_____

Solve.

5. Jeremy knows the surface area of a cube is 486 ft². Explain how he can compute the volume of the cube.

_____

_____

_____

_____

_____

6. Margot found the area of one of the faces of a cube to be 25 ft². Explain how she can use this information to find the volume and the surface area of the cube.

_____

_____

_____

_____

_____